H ey, what are you doing?" A deep voice almost blended with the sea as she whipped around. And then she felt herself slipping off the wet stone. In that same instant a firm hand grabbed her roughly by the arm and jerked her from the wall.

"You trying to get yourself killed?" His face loomed just inches from her own. She stared in silent shock at the penetrating eyes under thick brows. "Don't you know this is private property?" He gave her a slight shake, as if she were a small child caught stealing candy. She quickly studied him without answering.She could see he was a handsome man—almost frighteningly so!

She was trembling now. Mostly from cold. Still he gripped her arm as if he had no intention of letting go. What right did he have to detain her like this?

"Let go of me!"

Palisades.
Pure Romance.

FICTION THAT FEATURES CREDIBLE CHARACTERS AND

ENTERTAINING PLOT LINES, WHILE CONTINUING TO UPHOLD

STRONG CHRISTIAN VALUES. FROM HIGH ADVENTURE

TO TENDER STORIES OF THE HEART, EACH PALISADES

ROMANCE IS AN UNDILUTED STORY OF LOVE,

FROM BEGINNING TO END!

WISE MAN'S HOUSE

MELODY CARLSON

PALISADES

This is a work of fiction. The characters, incidents, and dialogues are products of the author's imagination and are not to be construed as real. Any resemblance to actual events or persons, living or dead, is entirely coincidental.

WISE MAN'S HOUSE
published by Palisades
a part of the Questar publishing family

© 1997 by Melody Carlson
International Standard Book Number: 1-57673-070-0

Cover illustration by Corbert Gouthier
Cover designed by Mona Weir-Daly
Edited by Lonnie Hull DuPont

Printed in the United States of America

For information:
QUESTAR PUBLISHERS, INC.
POST OFFICE BOX 1720
SISTERS, OREGON 97759

Library of Congress Cataloging--in--Publication Data
Carlson, Melody. The wise man's house/by Melody Carlson.
p.cm. ISBN 1-57673-070-0 (alk. paper) I. Title.
PS3553.73257W5   1997   96-50929
813'.54--dc21   CIP

97 98 99 00 01 02 03 — 10 9 8 7 6 5 4 3 2 1

To Christopher—
You are the romance in my life!
Thank you for being my anchor…
and the wind behind my sails.
I love you!

*Unless the L*ORD *builds the house,*
its builders labor in vain.

PSALM 127:1 (NIV)

↶ 1 ↷

Kestra McKenzie barely remembered driving from Portland to the coast. She pulled off the road and stared blankly at the old iron gate at the top of the hill. She could faintly make out the curved lettering across the top—Port Star Cemetery. She stepped out of the car and was met by cold, damp air. Now she remembered. She had come to talk to her mother.

She walked through the neatly kept graveyard and over the edge of the hill to where the grass was overgrown and weedy and the markers were small and insignificant. She knew this was crazy. What possible good could come from talking to her mother's grave? Lately, even her prayers sounded empty and pointless.

She pushed the weeds aside to reveal the smooth marble marker. She'd never seen the actual stone. Several years ago Jack had selected it from a design book in the monument store back in Seattle. They'd had it sent down to replace the small metal plate that had tarnished after a dozen years in Oregon's coastal weather. The marker was still nice and white. She traced her finger over the cold engraved lily. Kestra had never cared for lilies, but she'd kept this to herself. Jack was usually right about these things. And then when Jack died the following year, she'd requested that same lily for his stone. Now she wondered if he might have preferred something more masculine, like an oak tree or an elk. She stood and sighed. She was getting nowhere on this mission.

She stepped away from the grave and willed her mouth to open and pour out all the pent-up words, all the questions. But nothing came. She couldn't even formulate them in her mind. For the longest time she stood there blankly staring, waiting for something. But nothing happened, nothing changed.

She drove away slowly, almost dazed. She followed the curving coastal highway, focusing on the yellow lines, following one after the next. A horn blasted behind her. She was going too slowly. The truck honked again, long and loud this time. She should speed up, but she just couldn't. Finally she crept her car onto the shoulder and stopped as the trucker whooshed past and vanished into the fog.

She turned off the engine and leaned back, wishing she, too, could vanish. She imagined herself disappearing, swallowed up by the gray until she could see herself no more. Instead, she stared out into the fog and wondered when living had become so empty and pointless. Here she was, only twenty-eight years old, widowed for almost three years, and yet she was still stuck in Jack McKenzie's life. Day after day she went through the motions of what Jack would want her to do. Even later today in Portland, helping with the grand opening of another McKenzie's restaurant. And all for what?

She leaned her head against the steering wheel. If only she had someone to talk to. Someone older and wiser... "Please, God..." she whispered, not knowing what to ask, not knowing if God would want to listen. Maybe she was getting what she deserved.

She lifted her head and sighed.

"Grow up, Kestra McKenzie," she said as she turned on the engine and cranked up the window defogger. As the steamed windows slowly cleared, she noticed a familiar silhouette looming across the road. She'd almost forgotten it. It was the same old house, seated high on the bluff, that she and her mother used to pass on their way to and from church each Sunday. She used to pretend it was a castle, and of course, she was the beautiful princess who lived inside. Yet in all those years, she'd never ventured any closer than this to see it.

She put the car into drive and shot across the road, spinning gravel as she went. Today she would see it up close. She followed the long driveway clear up to the house and climbed out. The tall, steep-roofed three-story house looked dark and abandoned, and a few of its arched leaded windows were broken. The fog hung behind like an eerie backdrop, adding drama to its already forlorn appearance, but it did not frighten her. She had always thought this house was beautiful. At least three, maybe four, chimneys reached up to the dark sky like fingers of a hand pleading for help. She walked slowly around the sad old house, examining each sturdy stone wall. Built back before the turn of the century, it must have taken years to construct. Through various arched walkways she spied massive old doors hanging on crusty iron hinges. And in the back of the house, facing west, she spotted what appeared to be a beautiful, round stained-glass window up high, probably on the second floor. It seemed to be in one piece; in fact, most of the windows in back looked unbroken. She came around to the southwest corner to find an enclosed patio area. On a sunny afternoon it would be a delight. Too bad this wonderful old place had fallen into such neglect.

Finally she stopped by a low wall bordering the edge of what was probably once a garden, now overgrown with blackberries and ivy. She leaned over the wall to see what lay below.

A rocky cliff fell steeply to the ocean. She looked out to where the horizon of the sea must lie, but only saw a thick blanket of fog. Perhaps on a clear day… She sat upon a smooth, wide stone atop the wall, pulling her knees up to her chin and gazing down at the surf below. It smacked again and again into the black jagged rocks. Soon she grew mesmerized by the repetitious white foam, lulling her with its soothing rhythm as it pulled away, only to crash back again onto those immovable rocks. An occasional plume of spray shot straight over her head.

"Hey, what are you doing?" A deep voice almost blended with the sea as she whipped around. And then she felt herself slipping off the wet stone. In that same instant a firm hand grabbed her roughly by the arm and jerked her from the wall.

"You trying to get yourself killed?" His face loomed just inches from her own. She stared in silent shock at the penetrating eyes under thick brows. "Don't you know this is private property?" He gave her a slight shake, as if she were a small child caught stealing candy. She quickly studied him without answering. He was well over six feet tall, and she guessed him to be about thirty. His dark brown hair curled around his face attractively, and even behind his well-trimmed beard she could see he was a handsome man. Almost frighteningly so!

· She was trembling now—mostly from cold. He gripped her arm as if he had no intention of letting go. Then instantly and unexpectedly, she grew hotly indignant. What right did he have to detain her like this?

"Let go of me!" She shrieked, looking him straight in the eyes. She watched closely as his face registered surprise and his hand released her. He quickly stepped back, and she assessed her situation. Actually the man didn't seem dangerous. And yet she still felt her adrenaline rushing and her heart pounding as if it had a volume button turned up too high.

"I'm sorry I frightened you." His voice grew calm and quiet, almost soothing, as if she were a wild animal about to scratch his eyes out. Then she remembered what Jack used to say: "When Kestra's mad her hair gets redder and her eyes get greener." This thought, combined with the perplexed look on this handsome man's face, almost made her smile. Almost. She hadn't smiled in ages.

"I am truly sorry," he said again. "I thought you were one of those crazy high school kids. They hang around here and throw rocks through the windows and…" He shoved his hands into the pockets of his denim jacket and hunched his shoulders, turning his face toward the ocean, then back to her. "Actually, I thought you might fall. You probably didn't realize how these rocks can be slick when they're wet."

She nodded, appreciation sinking in. "I'm the one who should be sorry. I guess I'm trespassing. I didn't know anyone lived here. You see, I grew up in Port Star, and I've always wanted to come up to see this house, but I never did…until now. I'm really sorry to disturb you like this. Are you the owner?"

"No, I lease the caretaker's cottage. At least I did until—" He stopped and she looked at him. Of course, it was none of her business.

He continued. "Last fall some folks from Arizona bought the entire estate. They gave me notice last month. They plan to turn it into an inn or something."

"Oh, that'll be nice." She noticed his frown. "Well, not nice for you, I suppose…" She shivered.

"If you want, I just put on a pot of coffee. It might warm you up some." He tipped his head toward the small stone cottage. She hadn't noticed the tiny house before, but now she saw the windows glowing with yellow light and smoke curling from the chimney. She looked at his face again. It was a face like Michelangelo might have sculpted. Strong cheekbones, straight nose, smooth mouth. His eyes were dark brown, but now she

15

noticed the warmth of gold flecks, and the tiny fine lines along the edges revealed that maybe he actually smiled upon occasion. Something about him made her trust him.

"Sure, I'd like a cup of coffee."

She followed him up the brick path that led to the cottage, and he opened the door and she stepped inside. It was really quite charming in a messy sort of way. He shoved aside a pile of papers to clear a spot on the worn pine table. She noticed some seascape pencil sketches on top of the stack and wondered if he might be an artist. He looked like an artist. She could imagine him with an easel standing on a cliff painting the sea. She was curious, yet she felt she shouldn't ask, shouldn't intrude. Jack had always told her that a lady never asks too many personal questions of a new acquaintance.

Instead she talked about the weather. "Usually there's a brief warm spell in February," she said. "Sort of a false spring. I remember as a kid, just when I'd get my hopes up that it was time to wear shorts and go play on the beach, the old winter winds and rain would return with a vengeance."

He smiled. And it was one of those genuine smiles that made its observer feel warm and good. He refilled her coffee mug and replied. "We haven't had a false spring yet, but it would be a nice little change. Although I don't really mind the weather. I go out no matter what it's like. The wind and I get along real well." Again the smile.

"Have you seen any whales migrating yet?" She forced her eyes not to stare at his face, looking out the window, as if she were enjoying the view, only to be met by a blanket of fog. "Of course, it must be too early for whales…"

"Yes, not for a few more weeks at least. I guess I'll miss that when I leave. I sure will miss this place." He set down his mug and leaned forward.

"It's too bad," she said looking around self-consciously. "This must be a wonderful spot to live."

"It has been." He sighed. "It's been just what I've needed. But then it must be time to move on."

She wondered if that was a subtle clue for her. She looked at her cold, empty coffee cup. Her clothes were almost dry. She had no excuse to stay.

Rising, she said, "I'd better go." He stood and looked at her as if to say something, but no words came out. Then she glanced at her watch and remembered she had promised that she'd be back at the grand opening by seven tonight.

"Oh, my gosh! I've got to go. I didn't realize it was so late. I have to make it back to Portland in an hour!"

"Well, it looks like you've got just enough time."

Her hand flew to her hair, and she knew by touch that her curls had gone wild in the damp sea air. "I guess I'll make it, but I'll sure look like a mess!"

"You don't look like a mess to me," he said quietly, and his eyes crinkled a little at the corners—just the way she knew they would. She thanked him for the coffee, then reached for the doorknob, suppressing the desire to explain everything. If only she had more time. She felt like Cinderella, or maybe it was the White Rabbit. Mostly she felt silly.

She dashed through the fog toward her car, wishing for a reason to stay. Halfway to Portland, she realized she didn't even know his name.

～ 2 ～

"Kestra McKenzie, your condo is fantastic!" Holly dropped her overnight bag and ran her fingers through her short-cropped brown hair. "If I wasn't such a small-town girl, I'd be green with envy! I don't know why I never came to visit sooner. I swear, this is like something right out of *Lifestyles of the Rich and Famous.*"

Kestra forced a smile, longing to recapture that kind of enthusiasm.

"I'm so glad you came to visit, Holly. I've missed you so much. I meant to stop by last week when I was in Port Star. I really wanted to see your new shop. It's so great how you've started your own business. But then everything was so hectic with the restaurant grand opening in Portland and all..." She had no desire to tell Holly the real reason—about her stop at the old mansion. Something was so strange about her encounter by the sea that she felt to mention it would make it become common or trivial, erasing the mystique.

Holly pulled up the blinds in the living room and gasped. "I just knew it! Look at this view, it's amazing! How can you stand to leave your blinds closed?"

Kestra stared in surprise at the scene laid out before her living room window. There had been times when the Seattle lights had reminded her of glittering diamonds spilled across a length of dark blue velvet. Now they only looked cold and artificial. Yet for Holly's sake she nodded and smiled.

Holly kicked off her shoes and curled her toes into the lush, white carpet. Kestra remembered doing that same thing when she and Jack had first moved in, shortly after their wedding. Suddenly Holly turned and looked at her. "Kestra, you've changed," she said in an almost accusatory tone, then softened. "What's wrong? You seem so serious."

"Well, Holly, we all change. Just think, it's been almost ten years since I left Port Star and nearly three years since I last saw you." Actually, it felt like a lifetime ago.

"Yeah, and we've got tons of catching up to do. I'm only here till Sunday." Holly flopped down on the sofa. "This is nice, Kestra. I love the smell of leather."

Kestra nodded as she poured them tall glasses of clear soda over ice, laying a neat slice of lime on top just the way Jack had always done. "Thanks. Jack picked out most of the furnishings. Of course, I always liked his choices. Jack McKenzie had excellent taste. In furniture, food, clothes—well you name it—the man just plain had good taste. That's why his restaurants did so well. While he was alive, that is." Kestra took a long sip and leaned back.

"Meaning they're not doing so well now? How about that grand opening in Portland last week?"

Kestra shook her head. "Disaster. I think I wrote to you about how Jack left half the business to me and half to his son, Greg."

"Oh, yes—the bitter stepson, blames his wicked stepmother for all of his problems." Holly sounded like she was narrating a soap opera.

Kestra swirled the ice, watching it go slowly round and round the glass. She'd done everything she could to try to work with Greg, and yet preserve the integrity of Jack's business. She would have liked Greg's approval—if only for Jack's sake, but it seemed hopeless. Even when she let him handle the Portland grand opening his way and it flopped, he still blamed her.

"Come on, Kestra, help me out a little, I feel like I'm carrying this conversation all by myself. I don't get it—you used to be such a chatterbox. What's going on? It's almost like you're on sedatives. You're not are you?"

Kestra shook her head. Her doctor had prescribed something for the first few weeks after Jack's death. But the drugs had made her feel as if she had a thick gunny sack over her head, and she either slept too long, or not at all, and after a week she gave them up.

"And it's been nearly three years since Jack passed away. I know these things take a long time to get over, but—I'm sorry, Kestra, I shouldn't be so nosy…" Holly's words dwindled, as if she, too, had reached a dead end.

Kestra stared down at the massive oak coffee table, an antique she and Jack had unearthed in a little shop in Victoria B.C. She'd wanted it for their dining room, but instead Jack had gotten it cut down to use for a coffee table, and as usual he'd been right, it was perfect. She tried to think of the answer to Holly's question.

"I'm sorry, Kestra. Me and my big mouth. What do I know about grieving. It's just that you're only twenty-eight, and you live up here like a hermit. Do you go to church anymore? Do you ever date or anything? You act like you're an old woman, like your life is completely over." Holly leaned toward her, eyes wide with concern.

"Oh, Holly! I'm the one who should be sorry. Here, you've come for a fun weekend in the city, and I'm acting like a total mental case." Kestra forced herself to smile.

"I just want to see you happy, Kestra. But I really don't know what you need—"

"Maybe I just need you around to prod me, Holly. It's like I'm stuck or something. It's not so much Jack's death. Of course, that was difficult. But I think I'm mostly over it. But I just can't shake this gloomy cloud—do you know what I mean?"

Holly's brow wrinkled. Holly, the perennial optimist. How could she begin to understand what it was like to feel trapped or hopeless?

"And you know why I went to Port Star that day. I wanted to talk to my mother. Pretty crazy, huh? I drove like a maniac from Portland just to talk to her grave. And then I couldn't even do that."

"Well, that's not so crazy. But if you needed to talk to some-one, you could've come to me..." Holly's voice faltered.

"I know I could, Holly." Kestra looked into her friend's eyes. "You know, you've been the closest friend I've ever had. And yet even you don't know *everything* about me."

"Kestra, I know everything I need—"

Kestra cut her off. "Did you know the reason my dad left us was because he was a drunk and my mom threw him out? Did you know that the only way we survived was by living on tomato soup and macaroni? Did you know—"

Holly cut her off. "Oh, Kestra, you'd be surprised what I know. Remember Port Star's a small town. If you sneezed on Tuesday, Dr. Mitchell would hear you had pneumonia by Wednesday."

Kestra attempted a laugh, "Of course, what was I thinking? Everyone knew everything! Maybe that's why I worked so hard trying to prove something. Typical over-achiever trying to com-pensate for her diseased family tree."

"Come on, you sound like a self-help book! Over-achiever—

21

ha! And all this time, I thought you were just plain smart and tal-ented, although it never seemed fair you got the great looks, too!"

"Oh, Holly, you're too sweet."

Holly turned serious. "You know, Kestra, your mom would be proud of you."

Ever since that trip to the cemetery, Kestra had been trying to picture her mother's face. "Do you remember my mom, Holly? Do you remember how she looked?"

"Sure, I can still remember her behind the counter at Hartley's. I always thought she was real pretty. I hardly knew you back then, but I thought you were lucky to have such a nice-looking mom. Actually, she looked a lot like you, Kestra, only wasn't her hair brown? Yours is more auburn."

Kestra smiled at the description. "Honestly, you thought I was lucky?"

"Sure. Your mom seemed sort of glamorous to me. I mean, think about it, my mom was home in her housedress baking pies with curlers in her hair."

"I like your mom. And I used to envy you!"

"Kestra, you and your mom did the best you could."

"I know. But what do I do with this guilt?"

"What do you mean?"

"I mean, right before my mom died, I promised that I'd make something of myself—"

"And just look at you, Kestra. You're half owner of an upscale restaurant chain, and you live like a queen!"

"True. But I didn't do that myself. I *never* worked hard—I just got lucky! None of this has anything to do with me."

Holly frowned for a long moment. Kestra had seldom seen her at such a loss for words, and suddenly she was sorry for dumping on her like this.

"Kestra, sometimes you've got to let the past go."

"I know, and I thought I had. But after Jack died, it all

seemed to seep back into my life. Sometimes I think about what Mom would want me to do—then I think about what Jack would want me to do. I feel like I'm beating my head against the wall trying to make sense—"

"You'll never make sense of everything, Kestra. I don't mean to preach, but maybe you should ask God what you should do with your life." Holly held up her hands apologetically. "And on that happy note, how about if I go get freshened up. Aren't we going to McKenzie's for dinner?"

While Holly got ready for dinner, Kestra paced back and forth through her spacious living room, replaying parts of her life through her mind. What had she ever done that mattered? What had she accomplished? Sure she had finished flight attendant school. But why? Wasn't it only to snag a rich husband? Someone to take care of her and give her everything she'd always wanted? What would Holly think if she knew that? Was it even true? Hadn't she loved Jack?

Kestra sank into the big club chair—Jack's chair. He used to settle into it late in the evening and read his *Wall Street Journal*. She ran her arms over the smooth leather, tracing the piping with her fingertips. Of course, she loved him, she told herself, why else would she stay here and work so hard to keep these crazy restaurants going? Day after day, week after week, she fought against Greg to preserve Jack's business. It seemed her primary purpose in life was to keep everything just the way Jack liked it. Wasn't that love? Didn't that count for something?

Finally, Holly was ready and Kestra drove them to the restaurant, trying hard to make small talk along the way. She carefully steered the conversation away from the heavier topics. She didn't want to frighten Holly away. Holly was a friend worth keeping.

"This car is nice, Kestra. But how will you ever find a parking place? I haven't seen an empty spot since we left. Would it have been better to take a cab?"

Kestra laughed as she turned into the full parking lot at McKenzie's. "Not to worry, my dear." She drove through the lot to the back and pulled into a place marked 'Reserved for Jack McKenzie.'

They were warmly greeted at the door by Marcus, and he ushered them directly to a conspicuously empty table. The best table. People glanced up from their dinners as the two ladies were seated in their chairs. Within seconds, candles were lit, and a waiter appeared with a bottle of sparkling cider and graciously filled their glasses.

"I feel like a celebrity," laughed Holly. "I take it you told them you were coming?"

"Is everything all right, Mrs. McKenzie?" asked Marcus.

"Perfect, as usual." Kestra smiled up at the good man. He had been with Jack for many years before Kestra came along. Sometimes she wondered if he felt Jack's absence even more keenly than she. He bowed ever so slightly and slipped away.

"He treats you like Lady Di," whispered Holly.

Kestra lifted her glass and studied the bubbles. "I didn't order this, but I did tell them I'd be joined by an old friend tonight. I wonder if they thought it would be a man." To her surprise, thoughts of her mysterious stranger flashed through her mind. It had happened many times during the past week. She could remember every feature of his face and even the golden flecks in his eyes. It was a pleasant memory, although a little unnerving.

"Well, here's to old friends, anyway," said Holly as she clinked her glass to Kestra's. "Sorry I couldn't be some old flame for you."

Kestra laughed. "Glad that you're not. Right now I just need a friend."

"That's why I'm here." Holly smiled hopefully.

Kestra nodded and tried to pull herself back into the flow of

24

conversation, shoving the unexpected memory aside for now.

"Speaking of old flames, did you know that Dan and Melinda Hackett got divorced last year?" asked Holly. The waiter carefully placed a tempting selection of seafood appetizers between them and Kestra thanked him.

"These were Jack's favorites," said Kestra. "Try the smoked salmon pâté. That's too bad about Dan and Melinda. Don't they have kids?"

"Just one. A real brat actually. She takes after her mom." Holly tilted her nose up in a snobbish way.

Kestra forced a smile. "Melinda always had a certain air about her, didn't she?"

"I never did like her. And for the life of me, I never could figure what a nice guy like Dan saw in her."

Kestra lifted her brows. "Well, she was very pretty. And you just never can tell, she might have a good side."

"Okay, Kestra. But once and for all, I want the truth. If you don't want to talk about it, I'll shut up. But I have to ask."

"Go ahead, Holly, I'm an open book." Kestra stared evenly across the table. She had nothing to hide when it came to Dan Hackett.

"Okay then, when you left Port Star almost ten years back, were you hiding a broken heart? I mean you and Dan had gone together for a long time. I've never asked, but as your friend, I'd like to know."

"Well, to be perfectly honest, I was hurt. Think about it. Dan and I had only been apart for a couple of months. And even though I was the one who broke it off, I didn't expect him to get over me quite so quickly. And they were so young. Dan was barely twenty, and Melinda was only nineteen."

"Funny how that happens in small towns." Holly shook her head.

"I realize sometimes that it could've been me, and it's a very sobering thought. You know Dan had talked of marriage, but he always said he wanted to wait until he was around twenty-five. And then, of course, his parents never thought I was good enough…"

"Oh, brother!" Holly rolled her eyes. "I wish they could see you now."

"But honestly, Holly, looking back I wouldn't call it heart-broken. Even then I knew Dan wasn't the ultimate. I had this sneaking suspicion there was a whole 'nother world out there."

Holly looked around the restaurant. "You're right about that! Dan's pretty small potatoes compared to all this."

"Yes, but back then I wasn't totally sure. And when I left town, I did feel a little hurt and humiliated. I even wondered if Melinda might have been pregnant. She'd always had kind of a reputation. And we all knew she'd been after Dan for ages."

"Everyone in town thought so, too, but it turned out we were wrong." Holly spread some more pâté on bread. "It really was odd. I think maybe the parents arranged it all one night at the country club." She chuckled. "You know, Mrs. Hackett clears her throat and says, 'Dawling Mrs. Jennings, don't you think my wonderfully handsome Danny Boy would be a fine catch for your poor little Melinda?' And that's it, signed, sealed, and delivered right over martinis."

Kestra laughed over Holly's affected speech. It was perfect. "Holly, you're bad! Aren't you the one that's always preaching about how we're supposed to love our enemies?"

"Oh, I love them all right. I just can't stand how some people act. But now seriously, what would you think about Dan now? He still seems to be pretty nice. Melinda hasn't affected him too badly. Rumor has it, she's already moved on and is supposed to be pretty involved with her tennis instructor. But would you ever consider Dan—"

"Holly, for Pete's sake! I got over Dan Hackett ages ago."

"Okay, okay. I'm just trying to help. I thought maybe you needed a little romance to help snap you out of this blue funk, but I was probably wrong. Sorry, Kestra."

"I know you're just trying to help. Actually, I think I'm starting to see what my problem might be."

Holly leaned forward. "What?"

"Well, look around you." Kestra gestured to the restaurant. "See, these restaurants meant the world to Jack, and for the past couple of years, I've tried and tried to keep them going the way he wanted. But here I am partnered with his son. And Greg definitely has his own ideas. He wants to change everything."

Holly nodded. "What a lousy arrangement! It almost makes you wonder what Jack had in mind. Isn't Greg about your age, do you suppose—"

Kestra laughed. "Greg has had a girlfriend for some time. And I like her. I would like Greg, too, under different circumstances, although not romantically."

"Hmm, then I guess it's just a lousy arrangement."

"That pretty much sums it up." Kestra lowered her voice, carefully glancing around to make sure no one could hear. "And I have this guilty sense of responsibility that makes me feel like I must preserve everything for Jack. Like I don't really have my own life. I spend all my time asking myself, what would Jack want? What would Jack do? Of course, then I end up in huge fights with Greg because he wants everything different. But Jack always kept it all just like this—perfect."

"And why not, the food's amazing." Holly picked up a fork. "Beautiful silver, white linen, flowers, candles, the works. I love it."

"Right. And I say if it's not broken, why fix it? But Greg wants it to become less upscale—more of a regular place. Not only that, he wants to open more restaurants! He took some marketing class, and I honestly think he wants to start a new chain or something. You know, one at every freeway exit. We constantly butt heads, and I'm—" She cut herself off as the waiter reappeared with their salad. He carefully arranged them on the table, ground pepper, refilled glasses, and politely asked if everything was satisfactory. Kestra smiled and nodded.

"So why not just sell out?" asked Holly. "What's to stop you from just leaving?"

Kestra stared at Holly in amazement. How could she possibly think it would be so simple? "I can't just leave. How can I abandon everything that Jack worked so hard for?"

"Why not? After all, Greg is Jack's son, and Jack left him half the business. He must have thought Greg had some business sense. Besides, do you really want to live the rest of your life like this? And do you think Jack wanted you to be this miserable?"

Kestra shook her head. Jack had loved her, maybe even more than she'd loved him. He had tried to make up for her lousy childhood. She hated to admit it, but in many ways he'd been the father she'd never had. She swallowed a bite of salad over the lump in her throat. She did miss him.

"Look, Kestra, anyone can see you're unhappy. In fact, I'd say you're pretty close to being clinically depressed. There's hardly any life left in you. Where's that spunky little redhead with the flashing eyes, the one who was going to conquer the world? That's the woman Jack McKenzie fell in love with. Do you think he would want to see you like this?"

Kestra stared at the sputtering candle and the lovely long-stemmed rose, just the faintest shade of pink. She replayed Holly's words over and over—why not sell out? Why not?

Kestra looked up. "You're right, Holly. You're absolutely right."

Holly blinked in surprise. "Really?"

"Yes." Kestra laughed. "I can sell out. I don't have to stay here."

"And just think, Kestra, if you sell out your share of McKenzie's you could even start your own business." Holly's eyes lit up. "Hey, I just thought of something! Remember that old estate, you know that huge turn-of-the-century rock house you always liked—"

"You mean the old stone mansion on the bluff?"

"Yeah, that's it. Anyway, I just heard it's back on the market again. A couple wanted to make it into an inn or something, then suddenly changed their minds. You could—"

"Buy it!" Kestra dropped her fork and didn't even bother to look around to see if people were watching. "Do you think I could? Do you really think so?"

"Of course," laughed Holly. "I mean I don't see why not. I don't know how much money you have or anything—"

"Maybe I could make it into my own business. Maybe an inn, or a bed and breakfast, or maybe my own restaurant!"

"I suppose so—"

"You know, I have learned a lot about the restaurant business over the years. And I do like it. Let's see, Port Star is only an hour from Portland. That's good. I know I'd have to renovate. And of course, I'd have to sell my share of McKenzie's..." Already her mind was churning ahead. She tried not to think about the handsome stranger that might fit into this wild new dream. No, that was too much to consider right now. But in time, she would think about it. In time...

⌢ 3 ⌢

Kestra drove down the curving coastal highway, taking every opportunity to glimpse the clear blue on the horizon. For the first time in ages, she felt totally free. And it was a luxurious feeling that she was determined to hold on to as long as she could.

She took Holly's advice, and the following week had offered to sell her share of McKenzie's to Greg. He thought she was kidding. She assured him she was not. He said he couldn't pay full market price. She said that was fine. Now she hoped that wasn't a mistake. She also hoped it might change the way Greg remembered her. She had never understood his resentment toward her. It wasn't as if she had anything to do with his parents' split. His mother was already remarried long before she and Jack ever met. She hoped, for Jack's sake, that owning McKenzie's outright would help Greg.

Port Star was the same, yet different. She stopped by the new waterfront district. Unlike the rest of Port Star, it was colorful and interesting with artists' shops, dress boutiques, enticing coffee shops and bakeries, and even flower boxes already blooming with spring bulbs. She visited Holly and admired her shop packed full of antiques and decorative touches for home interiors. Holly was definitely in her element here. They agreed to meet later for dinner. Then she drove on over to Main Street.

Nothing in this part of town seemed much different: maybe a new sign over the barber shop, or that "T. J.'s Ice Cream Parlor" was now "T. J.'s House of Yogurt," but everything else looked just like high-school days. It was weird, as if she were still sixteen. She closed the door to her car and looked down the street in fascination.

"Howdy, Kestra!"

She froze. It was like a time warp. Same greeting, same raspy deep voice. She turned, and there he was sauntering towards her. He even looked the same, blond and tall. Dan's teeth still flashed white when he smiled, making a nice contrast to his tanned face.

"Kestra O'Brian, what a sight for sore eyes! Holly told me you were coming back to the old stomping ground." He stared hard, then slowly shook his head. "Things must've gone good for you Kestra girl, those are some mighty decent wheels." She felt relieved as he turned his attention to her car, smoothing his hand over the front fender of her sleek BMW. How irritating that after all these years, he could still make her feel like this. Well, she wouldn't let him get the best of her!

She stood up straight and laid her hand on the hood of the car, still warm from the engine. Jack had picked it out for her just before their third anniversary, and not long before his death. She would never have chosen silver, but Jack said he wanted her to have something flashy. She knew now that he had known he was dying then.

"Thanks, Dan, I can't complain," she said lightly. "But, for the record, I'm not O'Brian anymore. The name's McKenzie now."

"Oh, yeah. Hey, I was sorry to hear about your husband,

31

Kestra. Tough luck. I've had a little bad luck myself. But it's great to see you, and you really do look fantastic. I just can't believe you're back here in Port Star."

She didn't want to blush, didn't want to be taken in by this small-town-boy charm. She was above all that now.

"You look good, too, Dan. I'm sorry to hear about your split. Are you doing okay?"

"I'm doing great. 'Specially now that I've seen you. I swear, Kestra, you've just made my day. How long are you going to be around?"

"Well, I'm not really sure. I have to check something out." She glanced over her shoulder for the realtor's office. She remembered it being on Main Street somewhere.

"What are you checking out? Can I help you find anything?"

She smiled. He hadn't changed. Still nosy and bossy. Same old Dan. Nevertheless those ocean blues still took her by surprise, and for a moment she couldn't remember exactly why she'd returned.

"I'm looking for a Ms. Jan Smith, a realtor."

"Oh, sure, I'll take you right to her."

She stepped back, she didn't want Dan Hackett leading her around. People might think she'd come back because she'd heard about his divorce. She didn't need tongues wagging on her first day back. And if there was one thing she knew about Port Star, it was the way this town loved gossip.

"Oh, thank you anyway, Dan. I see the realty sign over there, I can find it now."

"But I'm happy to—"

"Thanks, just the same." She brushed him off and started across the street. It worked. Without looking back, she slipped into the little office.

Jan Smith was waiting for her and offered to drive out to the house, but Kestra suggested they meet. She told Jan she needed to get a bite to eat, and she'd see her out there at four, if that was okay. Jan didn't argue. Kestra figured Jan didn't sell houses in this price range every day.

Kestra was too excited to think about food as she drove straight to the house. She wanted to go there alone. Jan had explained why the couple was selling the estate; their marriage was on the rocks, and the prospects of turning the place into an inn had overwhelmed them. Kestra didn't mean to rejoice over their hardships, but she was thankful just the same. She hadn't asked about a certain tenant in the caretaker's cottage, and Jan had mentioned nothing, but Kestra felt certain he'd be there. It had only been a few weeks. And in her mind he belonged to the place. She wasn't exactly sure *why* she wanted to see him, or even what she'd say. She didn't even know his name. Yet those brief moments spent in his presence stayed with her, like the fleeting memory of a pleasant dream that didn't quite make sense. She had wanted an excuse to see him again. Today, she had it.

The weather remained clear except for a bank of fog suspended far out over the horizon. She parked halfway up the driveway and checked herself quickly in the mirror. Today her hair was perfect. She walked slowly up the drive, taking in each detail of the house and trying not to glance off toward that small stone cottage. In the sunlight, the house looked strong and immovable, perched like a sentry on its rocky bluff. She felt as if she were seeing it for the very first time, and she imagined that it was hers already.

The driveway was fairly long with a slight upgrade. Two stubby rock walls went along each side. There seemed to have been no attempt at any recent landscaping. The only visible vegetation on the bluff were gnarled and twisted trees shaped by the wind, clumps of Irish Broom, and gigantic mounds of blackberry bushes growing rampant and wild. She'd heard that at one time the original owners had kept a garden, supposedly enclosed by tall hedges to ward off the sea winds. But the property was too overgrown to even imagine where a garden could be hiding.

Three outbuildings were situated comfortably around the expansive house. Jan had told her the one toward the front was a carriage house, the one on the south was a stable, and of course, she already knew about the caretaker's cottage. Her heart beat a little faster as she glanced that way. There was no smoke from the chimney today, but then it was a mild day…

She stood on the moss-covered driveway and studied the huge house, willing her mind to focus and concentrate. She noticed now that, although the foundation and first floor were stone, it only continued midway to the second story. After that, weathered gray shakes went right up to the roofline. But the color was so similar to the stone, one hardly noticed the transition. Again she admired the arched leaded-glass windows. They were evenly spaced along the stone walls. It was definitely a house that lent itself to feelings of romance and mystique. She walked around the expansive circular porch that was centered in the front of the house. It rose up to a turreted roof and was flanked by another pair of turrets, starting on the second floor and blending into the roofline. She hadn't noticed the small dormer windows high in the roofline of the third floor. Jan had explained how the wings on each side of the house had been added in the twenties. But they melded easily into the overall design, which Jan had described as Queen Anne-Victorian, although Kestra wasn't quite sure if that was correct. Jack would have known. She suspected the house was a mixture of several styles, but she didn't care. To her, the house was perfect.

She had wondered if it might be smaller than she remembered, knowing how this often happens with childhood memories. But now she realized it was actually larger than she'd ever imagined. She knew it hadn't been lived in for several years and probably needed some serious work, but she wasn't worried. Jack had left her a comfortable life insurance settlement, plus she'd have what Greg had agreed to pay for her share of McKenzie's. Money wasn't a problem.

She didn't need the realtor to talk her into this. She already knew. She wanted this house.

~ 4 ~

Kestra became so captivated by the house she almost forgot about the caretaker's cottage and its tenant. Almost. At first, she had expected him to pop up on her, to catch her by surprise. That's the way she had hoped it would happen. But when it didn't, she decided to walk down the trail toward the small cottage and look around. She paused at the rock wall. The same wall he'd rescued her from when she'd started to slip.

No lights glowed from the cottage today. She knocked on the wooden door, and a chunk of peeling paint fell off. No one answered. She peered in the window. It looked much the same as she remembered, except there were no traces of human habitation. He was gone. Cold disappointment washed over her, and in the same instant, she chided herself for reacting emotionally. Only a fool would lament for a man she hardly knew. He was probably a drifter. But still, the memory of those golden-flecked dark eyes haunted her. Perhaps she should simply savor that memory and allow this unrealistic hope to die a peaceful death. After all, there was still the house.

It was half past three when Kestra heard the car pull into the drive. Jan must have come early, but Kestra didn't want to see

36

her yet. She'd discovered the perfect niche—a protected stone patio, tucked into the south corner of the house—and she didn't want to be disturbed. The patio overlooked the sea and provided a haven for daydreaming, something Kestra had almost forgotten how to do. Even with the wind blowing, she was sheltered, and the afternoon sunlight poured in its warmth. Already she was envisioning this spot with nice patio furniture, some potted flowers—

"Hey, Kestra, where you hiding?" She recognized the voice, definitely not Jan's. What in the world was Dan Hackett doing out here? "Ah-ha, I found you! Should've known I'd catch you soaking up the sun. You always were a heat freak."

"Dan, what are you doing?" She didn't attempt to cover her exasperation. "And how did you know I was here, anyway?"

"Oh, I just ran into Jan Smith at the coffee shop. I mentioned how I'd pointed you her way, and, well, the rest is history. So what do you think of the old wreck? You aren't seriously considering buying this heap of trouble, are you?"

If he'd insulted her dead mother, he couldn't have offended her too much more. She rose to her feet, fists clenched. "I'll have you know, Mister Know-It-All, I happen to love this 'old wreck.' This is a grand house, and even though it's absolutely none of your business, yes, I do intend to buy it, maybe even today!"

Dan held up his hands. "Whoa—slow down, little lady. Take it easy!" He grinned. "Hey, now that's like the old Kestra I used to know. You've still got fire in those eyes."

She didn't like his smile. She folded her arms across her front and scowled, saying nothing.

"And excuse me all to pieces for insulting your house like that, Kestra. Really, the only reason I came out was to offer my professional opinion. I'm a building contractor, and I'm pretty familiar with remodeling. Of course, if you want, I'll just mosey

on my way. I was just willing to share some free expertise..."
He turned his back but didn't walk away.

"I thought you were still in the lumber business with your dad?" It sounded more like an accusation than a question, but she wasn't ready to forgive him, plus she didn't quite believe he'd come out to help.

"Nah, haven't you people in Seattle heard about our sacred spotted owl down here? That little critter, and several others, have managed to lock up our woods so the best we can do is pull out a twig now and then. I decided a few years back to find another racket. But I still love the smell of fresh cut wood. So here I am, Dan Hackett Construction, at your service." He took off his hat and bowed.

"Very cute, Dan. Okay, tell me what you think. What's your professional opinion?"

He slowly ran his eyes up and down and across, then whistled long and low. It didn't sound good.

"You got plenty of money, Kestra?"

"What do you mean by plenty?"

"Well, you know what this place is selling for?"

"Of course, I do!" She drew in a sharp breath. "What—do you think I'm an idiot?"

"Now settle down, I'm just trying to help." He looked sincere as he continued. "Okay, you know how much this place costs... Now, you can just about double that figure. It'll cost about that much." He eyed her. She didn't flinch. *Yes*, she thought, *I can do this!*

When Jan got there, the three of them began to tour the house. The front entryway was wide and open with the ceiling soaring up to the top of the third story. It had an old slate floor that looked like there was plenty of life left in it. Off to the left was a library, complete with floor to ceiling bookshelves and a big fireplace framed in an old wood mantle. Dan mentioned that the hardwood floor was creaking under their steps, but to Kestra it was a friendly sound. Dan acted as if he were an integral part of the whole process, offering his comments freely, what was good, what was not. He made it very clear that the kitchen would need massive work and updating to bring it to restaurant standards. But she pointed out how nice the dining area was with old red fir floors and a bank of windows, and there were a couple of rooms that could be opened up to make the dining room larger. Dan questioned whether it would be possible or not, and how one wall was probably a weight-bearing wall. Kestra appreciated his advice but grew increasingly irritated at his controlling attitude. It seemed every time she praised something, he wanted to tear it apart.

As they climbed the old, curving wood staircase to the second floor, Kestra commented on the lovely hand carving.

"It's a fine work of craftsmanship," agreed Jan. "Nothing around here compares to it. This house is truly one of a kind."

"Oh, look!" Kestra pointed to a glowing circle of colored light. "I saw the stained glass window from outside. It's so beautiful, look at those rich jewel tones."

"Probably sucks the heat right out of the house," said Dan. He turned to Jan. "What's the square footage up here anyway?"

"I don't know offhand." Jan looked puzzled.

"Well, can you find out? Don't you have an electronic measuring device?"

She reached into her purse. "Sure, just a minute." Then Dan scooted Kestra off into a bedroom at the end of the hall.

"Listen, Kestra, you're doing this all wrong."

"What do you mean?"

"For one thing, you're showing way too much interest here. You're letting her lead you around by the nose. You need to act a little skeptical. If you really want this place, don't let it show, unless you want to pay top dollar that is."

Aha, the light went on. "You mean, I might be able to get it for less?" They heard Jan's footsteps coming down the hall, and he continued in a whisper.

"Of course. Haven't you ever heard of making an offer? Just because it has a price on it doesn't mean they expect to get it." His voice grew lower and she leaned closer to hear. She felt his breath on her cheek and, to her dismay, felt a shiver go down her back. "The thing is," he continued, "act like you're going to walk, like you don't really need this place. Like it's a lot of work, and maybe you don't want to be bothered. Then you make a lower offer, maybe even fifty thousand lower."

Her eyes widened. "Go down that much? Really? For this type of house? The price is pretty reasonable already."

He shook his head and placed his hand on her shoulder. "Listen, Kestra, I've heard the owners are having serious financial problems, and they need to unload it quick. Besides, they can always counter your offer."

"Counter?" She felt her knees trembling and wished he'd remove his hand from her shoulder. This was way too close for comfort. Jan was milling around in the doorway now, and Dan slipped his arm around her and guided her toward the window. Obviously a tactic to cut Jan off, or maybe something more.

"A counter offer," he whispered, "is when the owners come back with an amount somewhere between your offer and the original price."

"Oh, I see. Thanks." She quickly moved out from under his arm and walked toward the door. "Oh, Jan, we didn't mean to leave you out. My friend Dan is just explaining how much work this place needs. I simply had no idea." She hoped Jan picked up on the word *friend*. All she needed was for this woman to return to town with stories about them.

"Well, yes, of course it needs work. It's old. It needs some T.L.C.—"

"Or T.N.T.," chuckled Dan.

Jan glared. "With a little work, it could be quite wonderful. I have those measurements if you're really interested," she said coolly.

Dan nodded and Jan launched into numbers that Kestra didn't care to hear. She wandered on down the hallway, inspecting each room. It was plain to see that there was plenty of space. She had already counted seven bedrooms on this floor alone. She had no idea what she would even do with them. But she knew which one would be hers. She stared in amazement at the spacious room. It must have been the master suite with its large closets, dressing room, and private bath. Most importantly it had a wide bank of windows complete with a beautiful view of the ocean. She looked out across the sea of blue and sighed. It was perfect. Reluctantly she left the room to find Jan and Dan in the hallway. Jan had a perplexed look on her face as Dan continued to bombard her with questions.

"Do you know anything about the wiring?" he asked.

"Well, I think it's still pretty old in places, but there are parts that have been rewired in recent years." Jan shifted her gaze from one to the other.

"How about the plumbing?" he continued like a heckler.

She pressed her lips together, plainly irritated. "Well, it, too, is old, but that doesn't necessarily mean it needs to be replaced. I just sold a seventy-year-old house, and the plumber said it was better than some of the houses built ten years ago. The fact is, this house is a one-of-a-kind beauty. Obviously, you aren't buying it for all its modern amenities."

Kestra was starting to feel sorry for Jan, and cut Dan off before he continued his interrogation. "I'm interested in making an offer," she said.

Jan smiled, turning her full attention to Kestra. "Well, shall we return to my office to write it up? I have another gentleman coming by this evening, he's also interested in this property. Perhaps we should write up your offer this afternoon, in case he wants to make an offer as well."

Kestra grew anxious. What if someone else got this house? What if she took Dan's advice and made an offer that was too low, and someone snatched it away from her?

"Shall we meet at my office, say at five-thirty, then?"

"That's fine," agreed Kestra. She must have this house.

"Uh-oh, look at the time," said Dan. "I've gotta meet my concrete man at five to discuss tomorrow's job. I better beat it. See you later, Kestra. Bye, Jan."

"I've got to run, too, Kestra. See you at five-thirty." Jan squeezed her hand.

They both were gone and Kestra stood alone before the house of her childhood dreams. The wind lightly tossed her hair, and she remembered how much she loved this unpredictable coastal weather. The sun was getting low in the sky, and she pulled her jacket about for warmth.

What should she do? Take Dan's advice and make a lower offer? Pay the full price? She stared up at the house, wanting it desperately. She'd never asked God to give her such specific direction before. Usually her prayers were vague, asking for strength, general guidance, and things you couldn't measure or weigh. Dare she ask God for a specific number? It seemed awfully presumptuous, maybe even sacrilegious. And what if God didn't want her to have this house? She took a deep breath and prayed. If she were to have this house, she wanted it to be founded on God. He was the only immovable rock. And right now she needed that kind of solidity in her life.

∼ 5 ∼

To her amazement, a figure for the price came to her. It was more than Dan had suggested, but still a bit less than the asking price. She told Jan the amount with confidence and sat and watched as her offer was typed up and placed in a sealed envelope. Even when Jan reminded her about the gentleman looking at the property that very evening, Kestra didn't waver. If her offer was refused, she'd accept it as God's way of saying the house wasn't meant for her. But somehow she knew that wouldn't be the case.

"I can't believe you, Kestra," exclaimed Holly over dinner. "You just up and make a cash offer on a huge estate, and then sit here so calm and cool. I'd be going absolutely nuts! In fact, I think I'm more excited than you are! I guess I still feel a little responsible. After all, I'm the one who enticed you over here by telling you about the place. Will you hold it against me if you get it, and it turns out to be a disaster?"

Kestra laughed, "Of course not, silly. And for the record, I am absolutely numb with excitement. But something about this all just feels so right that I don't feel nervous."

"Well, feelings can be misleading."

"Believe me, Holly, I know." She remembered her feelings for the stranger. "But there are feelings, and there are feelings."

"Uh-huh, I understand. It's like when I decided to quit my teaching job. I took out all my savings and went in with the others to buy the old cannery on the waterfront. My folks thought I'd lost my marbles. But look how well it's turned out, and all because of a hunch. And I really couldn't be happier with my life." Holly paused, then continued wistfully, "Well, maybe a little—maybe if Mr. Right came along and swept me off my feet."

"Are you still looking for Mr. Right, Holly? Don't you know by now that's just some old wive's tale?"

Holly laughed. "Yeah, probably some miserable old wife who wanted to spare the rest of us, so she made up this wonderful tale about finding the perfect man, the one that doesn't exist, right?"

"I suppose..." Again Kestra thought of the stranger. She wished she could get him out of her mind. "But it was a nice fairy tale, at least when we were little."

"I thought when you married Jack, you'd found your Mr. Right. Although, I admit, the age difference was hard to accept at first. But you seemed happy, and he was so nice, so handsome, and he was even rich."

"Yes, Jack was a very special guy."

"But not Mr. Right?"

Kestra sighed. "I guess I just don't believe in that Mr. Right business. But Jack was wonderful, and he was always good to me. He was dependable. I needed someone like that. But, Holly, if I ever marry again, there's got to be something more. Not only will I have to like and respect him, but there'll have to be some pretty amazing fireworks!"

Holly nodded. "I totally agree." She lifted her coffee cup as if in a toast, "Here's to fireworks." They clicked cups and giggled.

"Excuse me, is this a private party?" interrupted an all-to-familiar male voice. Kestra looked up to see Dan. He no longer wore his work clothes, but was now attired in a light blue chambray shirt and neatly pressed khaki pants.

"Hi, Dan," said Holly with a smile. She pulled out a chair, then Kestra noticed another man lingering behind Dan.

"This is Matthew," introduced Dan, pulling out another chair. "Can we intrude and buy you lovely ladies some dessert? The deep-dish blackberry pie is great. Especially for us bachelors. Next best thing to home cooking." He winked at Kestra. "You baked me a blackberry pie once, remember."

"Ugh, don't remind me. I'm still pretty hopeless in the kitchen." Kestra tried to keep her tone light, but just the same, she didn't want to go down memory lane with Dan.

"Well, I'm not ashamed to admit, my culinary skills have improved a lot over the years," announced Holly. "Of course, it took a few cooking classes down at the community center, and I can't tell you how many times I've set my smoke alarm off with some of my burnt sacrifices." Holly directed her conversation to Matthew. "Matthew, you're a new face. What brings you to Port Star, and how did you ever hook up with the likes of Dan Hackett?"

Matthew grinned. He had brown wavy hair that curled down the back of his neck, and his eyes looked to be a grayish shade of blue. *Oddly like Holly's,* thought Kestra. He wore a plaid shirt with sleeves rolled up to the elbows.

"Well, Dan and I are connected by way of a business relationship," said Matthew. "He wanted to buy me a drink, but since I don't go in for the bar scene, he was forced to bring me over here for dessert instead. Not a bad idea as it turned out."

"What business are you in?" asked Kestra, not really curious, but hoping to divert her conversation from Dan.

"Concrete." He answered. "I operate out of Harrison. Ever heard of Porter's?"

"Oh, sure," exclaimed Holly. "I've seen the Porter trucks around. I love those bright rainbow stripes on their cement trucks. I've always wanted to tell Mr. Porter what a great idea that was."

"Well, you just did," said Matthew modestly. "Thanks. Some of my guys give me a hard time about my rainbows, but you know, the kids really love them. Besides, I always considered the rainbow to be a sign of hope. Seems to me this world could use a little more hope, don't you think?"

Both women stared at Matthew. Kestra thought this guy was incredible, and she could tell Holly thought the same.

"So, Kestra," said Dan, changing the subject. "How'd your real estate deal go. You make an offer?"

She turned her attention reluctantly to Dan. "Yes, in fact, I did." She wasn't eager to discuss her offer, but she knew Dan wasn't going to let her off.

"Did you take my advice?"

"Partly. But I came up with my own amount."

"I bet you went too high. You'll just be wasting your money, Kestra. You should have let me help you."

There was no way she was going to explain how she'd prayed, and how God seemed to answer. Dan wouldn't understand. She glanced at Holly. She and Matthew were engaged in conversation. Once again Kestra was stuck with Dan. It was irritating how he'd managed to monopolize her attention for the better part of the day.

"Well, anyway I hope it wasn't too much," he continued. "You know, it's gonna take an awful lot just to make the place livable."

She sipped her coffee and felt herself roll her eyes at him. It was a childhood habit that Jack had tried to break her of many a time. Apparently Dan didn't notice.

"First, you'll need to get that roof repaired. Most of it's shot, but there might be some portions that can be saved. Those are a different style of shake shingles, but I know a guy in Long View who can get them for us. Also, there's sure to be some dry rot."

She sat down her cup and looked at him with a small flicker of interest. It seemed he'd actually put some thought into her house. "What is dry rot, anyway?" she asked.

He continued to explain, and this time she listened carefully, taking it all in. He almost seemed to have a work plan for her house. If it *was* her house, that is.

"Well, I hate to break up such a nice party," announced Matthew, looking at his watch. Kestra realized she'd nearly forgotten about Matthew and Holly, she'd been so engrossed in house talk.

"Yeah, we working boys have to be up early." Dan rose from his chair and stretched. "Let me know how your bid turns out, Kestra." He touched her shoulder.

"Nice meeting you both," said Matthew. He turned to Holly. "And I'll stop by and see this shop of yours some time. It sounds interesting. Evening." He picked up the check and the two guys left.

"Wow," breathed Holly. Kestra thought she saw stars in her friend's eyes.

"Is it fireworks?" asked Kestra, with a slight twinge of jealousy.

"Could be." Holly's voice sounded dreamy, and there was definitely a far-off look on her face. This was not a typical Holly response, not in the least.

"Hey, Matthew took our dinner check," noticed Kestra. "Do you suppose he meant to do that?"

"Wouldn't surprise me, Kestra. There's not too much about that guy that would surprise me. And guess what else."

"What?"

"He's a Christian."

"Oh, that's really super, Holly!" Kestra meant it. For Holly's sake, she hoped there might be something to this. Matthew did seem like quite a guy.

"Looks like you and Dan are hitting it right off."

"Bite your tongue, Holly! Dan and I were simply talking business. He is, after all, a building contractor. He knows a lot about renovating old houses."

"My, my, no need to get all hot about it. Besides, Kestra, he didn't look all business to me."

"Well, just for the record, I am only interested in Dan Hackett for his professional advice—period. Understand?"

"Yes, ma'am. And just for the record, I am extremely interested in Matthew Porter—and it has nothing to do with cement!"

They laughed. Kestra knew this was Holly's way of warning that, for the time being, Matthew was off-limits. Kestra didn't want a man in her life right now anyway. Not even her mysterious stranger. Right now she wanted to focus on her house. She wished she knew for sure how her offer was being received. In her mind, the house was hers, and she could already envision the roof being repaired. Unfortunately, that picture also appeared to contain Dan Hackett. He did know a lot about fixing houses, and he did seem very interested in helping with hers. She just hoped it wasn't more than that.

6

Hi, Jan," Kestra tried to conceal her eagerness as she spoke into the phone from Holly's apartment. "I know it's only been a couple days, but I wanted to check to see how it's going with my offer."

"Hello, Kestra." Jan sounded professional. "Well, it's taking a little longer. The couple who own the estate are separated. The husband's in Arizona, and I'm not sure about the wife. I Fed-Exed your offer to Phoenix. Of course, you should know the gentleman from California made an offer as well."

Kestra closed her eyes and took a breath. "I don't suppose you can tell me what he offered…"

"No, of course not. But I should let you know, you are allowed to make a second higher offer. Not that I'm suggesting his offer was more. I only want you to realize it's within your rights to do so."

"Yes, I see. Thank you, Jan. I'll give it some thought and get back to you." She hung up the phone and sank into Holly's big easy chair. What now? It was probably a good thing Holly was at the shop, that way Kestra could think undisturbed. This wasn't a decision to make lightly. She picked up her coffee mug and took a sip. The coffee was cold. She leaned back and stared up at the ceiling. Should she make a higher offer?

She prayed in silence, begging God to show her once more. Maybe a higher number… She wanted the house so much. But no new figure came. What if God didn't want her to have the house after all?

She paced back and forth in Holly's tiny living room, arguing with herself. Or was it with God? Maybe she should just offer the full asking price. Maybe she should offer a little bit more. She wanted that house.

The house was built on a rock, and she wanted to rebuild her life on a rock. Her rock was God. If she was going to get the house, she must trust him. Even if it meant losing the house, she would stand firm. God would take care of things, she just knew it.

To distract her thoughts, she busied herself by cleaning and straightening Holly's tiny apartment. It was so great of Holly to let her stay with her until she got things figured out. Kestra hoped it wouldn't be for long. She plumped a rich-colored tapestry pillow and leaned it against the chair. Holly had a knack for decorating that was reflected in her home as well as in her interior decor shop. Kestra observed the antiques and collectibles that filled each room, accented by baskets and rugs and unusual items. Yet it didn't look overly cluttered, just interesting and comfortable—a lot like Holly.

Kestra wondered how she would decorate her own place. She'd never really had the chance to pick out things before. Jack had always done that, and although she liked his taste, there were times she'd have done it differently. Before she'd left Seattle, she'd quickly stored all their belongings to sort out later, after she got settled.

Tonight, Holly had invited Matthew and Dan over for dinner. Kestra was happy about Holly's interest in Matthew, but didn't appreciate being included as a foursome, especially paired off with Dan. He made her uneasy. Sometimes it seemed like he just assumed they were right where they'd left off ten years ago, and so far, he hadn't even mentioned Melinda or his eight-year-old daughter. But then, she didn't really want to hear about that. Mostly, to her relief, they talked about the house.

Kestra drove to the house that afternoon. She knew it would help calm her. The sky was foggy and gray, a lot like the time she'd met the stranger, but she tried not to think of him. Today she was dressed for ocean weather with her faded blue jeans and fisherman-knit sweater. Jack had bought the sweater for her from a small Irish shop during their last vacation. He'd tried to talk her out of it, urging her to take the pretty shell-pink cashmere instead, but she'd stubbornly insisted on the heavy fisherman knit. The shopkeeper had thought Kestra was his daughter. Kestra had thought it was funny, but it had irritated Jack. She didn't know then that Jack was dying of cancer, but looking back, she realized he had known. The spur-of-the-moment vacation must have been a result of his hopeless diagnosis. It was a swift-acting liver cancer, the kind for which the doctors didn't recommend treatment. At least Jack hadn't suffered long. He was on so much pain medication in the end that he was oblivious to almost everything, even Kestra.

She stepped out of the car and welcomed the cold mist to her face, shaking the haunting memories from her mind. It was time to move on, and the house seemed like her ticket to do so. She looked up at it, so regally perched and rock solid. It had been there long before her and would in all likelihood remain long afterwards. Maybe she would help it to remain. Her mind flashed back to the time she'd secretly named this house. She'd never told anyone. It had been a Sunday on the way home from church. She'd been sitting next to her mother in the dusty little Toyota, waiting for the house to appear around the next corner, and thinking about the story she'd just heard in Sunday school. It was the story of the Wise Man and the Foolish Man. They'd both built houses, but the Foolish Man had built his on the sand. She couldn't imagine why anyone would build a real house on the sand. She had built enough sand castles and watched them wash away with the tide to know that wasn't a very good idea. But the Wise Man had done it right. So on that day, about twenty years back, she secretly renamed the house on the bluff, 'The Wise Man's House.'

She circled the entire house and tried to memorize each line, each turret, each window. Finally she came to the back and settled on the sheltered south-west corner patio. Most of the house was in serious need of repair, but the south wing seemed to be in the best shape. She wondered if she might possibly live in this section, while the rest was being restored. Or perhaps she would stay in the caretaker's cottage. She decided to give the cottage a closer look. Of course, she'd been inside once, but she'd been so captivated by her host that now she barely remembered the actual living conditions of the cottage.

There was no denying it was a charming little house, and it even had its own ocean view. She walked around to the back and was surprised to find the back door slightly ajar. She didn't remember it being open before. She stepped inside with some hesitation, but then realized she might soon be the owner and for that reason had every right to look around. The interior smelled musty, like old wood and damp sea air, but not an entirely unpleasant aroma. Nothing a few weeks of warm fires couldn't take care of. The wide-planked floor creaked gently as if welcoming her. The cottage consisted of a large front room and a small bedroom with a tiny bathroom tacked off the side. The furnishings were worn and sparse but could easily be replaced. Maybe she would do something with rustic cabin-style furniture. Holly would help her find some cute things.

The front room also contained a small kitchenette. Its floor was covered in peeling linoleum, straight out of the thirties. But the solid wood cabinets looked sturdy. She tried the tap at the old porcelain sink. First the water came out brown, but it finally ran clear. Yes, she could easily make do here with a bit of work. It would be fine for a temporary shelter. She considered what Jack would think of such primitive lodgings. Would he think she was a complete fool? He was always used to the best.

She was about to leave when she noticed a metal foot locker tucked behind the sagging old couch. She tried to open it, but it was locked. It felt heavy, and she wondered what it might contain. Did it belong with the cottage, or might it possibly be something the stranger had left behind?

She stepped out, wishing she could lock the door, but knew it was impossible without a key. She'd call and mention it to Jan. She didn't want transients camping here in her house. She rounded the corner of the cottage and nearly ran into him.

Her heart lurched, and she knew her face registered her shock. She hoped that was all her expression revealed.

"Hello there. I'm so sorry, I didn't mean to startle you," the stranger touched her arm, and then quickly removed his hand. "I thought I recognized your car just now. You see, I was picking up some things I'd left here, then I went to town to check on something. Now I'm back and here you are."

"You just took me by surprise." The words came out breathlessly, and Kestra fought to regain composure.

"I seem to have a habit of that." He smiled and the fine lines appeared around his eyes again. Same flecks of gold. So reassuring. So unreal.

"You know," Kestra said, "the last time we met, I never got your name."

"I'm sorry. How rude, and all this time I've known yours— Kestra—Kestra McKenzie, right?"

She nodded. She didn't remember giving her name.

"My name's Quin Larson." He extended his hand, as if to make the introduction official. She took it, and it was warm and strong. She wished her hand weren't so cold. He held it for a long moment, as if to let the warmth seep in. Then, self-consciously, she pulled away and felt her cheeks glow. The wind always made her face flush, perhaps he wouldn't notice. *Quin Larson,* she repeated the name in her mind. Perfect.

"I wish I could offer you a warm fireplace and a hot cup of coffee again, but as you can see, I don't live here anymore."

"Yes, I noticed—a few days ago."

"You mean you've been here?"

She felt the need to make everything clear. She didn't want him to think she was hunting him down, even if it was partly true. "I came to have another look at this house."

"I see…" He looked over to the house and nodded with appreciation. "Yes, it's quite a place."

"I suppose you've heard the couple who bought it have placed it back on the market again."

He nodded. "Yes. I had already made plans to return to California at the time or I might've considered asking to stay on."

"So you're from California?"

"I'm not really *from* California. I'm just staying there awhile to take care of some things. I guess I'm sort of drifting right now."

She studied him. He just didn't look like a drifter. Today he wore a thick tweed jacket, heavy cords, and hiking-style leather boots—he could have been on the cover of an Eddie Bauer catalog. She glanced over his shoulder to the driveway. Next to her car was a late model Land Rover—certainly not the vehicle of a drifter.

Despite her warm sweater, the cold damp had seeped

through, and she felt herself give an involuntary shiver. Just the same, she'd happily turn blue, anything to keep this moment from ending.

"Say," he said. "There's a little chowder house down the road. Have you had lunch yet?"

"Actually I was so absorbed by the place, I forgot all about eating."

"Come on, then. Let me buy you a bowl of the best chowder, at least within the radius of, say, about ten miles."

"You don't make the cuisine sound too tempting, but as long as it's hot, I don't mind."

He laughed. It was a quiet sort of laugh. Some might not have classified it as a laugh at all, but to Kestra, it sounded sincere. This time she wasn't about to dash off like the White Rabbit. For him, she had all the time in the world.

~ 7 ~

They drove separately to Gil's Chowder House. She hadn't been there for years, and it wasn't a place she'd have chosen. And not just because of the smoky atmosphere or tacky decor. The last time she'd been there had been with her father. She had shoved that memory down as she'd driven. After all, that was another lifetime ago—and nothing was going to spoil this day for her. Quin met her at the door, and a middle-aged waitress greeted him by name and led them to a booth next to a salt-sprayed window overlooking the surf. The waitress' polyester uniform strained at the buttons and her apron was stained, but she smiled as she flopped the menus down on the oil-cloth wrapped table.

"Quite a joint, isn't it?" Quin grinned a crooked grin. But the greasy dive could have been the Ritz Carlton for all Kestra cared. He continued, "I know this place lacks a little refinement, but the view's good, and the people who hang out here have always interested me—this place attracts some real characters. And like I said, they do make a mean bowl of chowder. I hope you don't mind."

"Of course not. And you forgot to mention, it's warm." She rubbed her hands together.

Quin waved at the waitress, "Say, Mertie, how about some hot coffee over here?"

"Coming right up, Sweetheart," she called, grabbing two thick stoneware mugs and a pot. In the next instant she was pouring coffee and taking their order for two bowls of chowder and homemade bread.

Kestra excused herself to go to the ladies' room, which was the size of a small closet and in need of a good scrubbing. She peered self-consciously into the mirror. The bathroom light was dim and the mirror was foggy with age. She wondered what Quin thought of her looks. It felt strange and a little juvenile to care. She touched her windblown hair, a mass of tangled curls. Any attempt with a comb would be useless. Her cheeks were flushed from the wind, but it did add some color to her face.

On her way past the kitchen, she noticed the carving of the old fisherman. Of course, it would still be there. And of course it would bring back every vivid detail of that horrible night when she was here with her father. The whole scene flashed before her mind's eye in the time it took to walk across the room.

It was her tenth birthday, and her mother had to work late. Dad came home that night with whiskey on his breath and announced they were going to Gil's to celebrate. They sat at a table in the middle of the crowded room, and her dad put away several beers, until he got, what her mother would have called, "a little feisty." Kestra had wanted to crawl under the table as his voice grew louder and louder demanding their food. Finally he charged the kitchen, knocking over the carved statue, and letting loose with a stream of language that might have made the wooden fisherman blush. The owner, Leroy Gilbert, threw him out the front door, and she sneaked out the back.

She noticed Leroy as she slipped back into the booth. He was still behind the high counter, older and grayer. He probably didn't remember the incident. She slipped into the booth, willing herself back into the present.

"Is something wrong, Kestra?" Quin's eyes looked concerned.

"Oh, not really." She wanted to dismiss the silly memory and focus instead on Quin.

But he continued to look with such kind eyes that she wondered if he might understand. She picked up the heavy coffee mug and wrapped her hands around it, trying to absorb its heat.

"Oh, I just had this silly flashback. It's this cafe. You see, I have been here before. I think I mentioned to you about growing up in Port Star..."

He nodded, not taking his eyes off hers. She studied the flecks of gold that warmed his eyes. He seemed to look right through her, but not in a bad way—more like he was searching for something.

"My dad brought me here once when I was a kid. He was an alcoholic, and as usual, he'd had a few too many and made a complete fool of himself—and me." Somehow she felt better for saying it. Just hearing the incident formed into words made it seem less shameful and horrible. She laughed nervously. "See? I told you it was silly. No big deal."

"No, it's not silly. And I'll bet you still felt humiliated by the memory."

"Yes, that's it. Exactly."

"Isn't it funny how, as adults, we can still blame ourselves for things we had no control over in our childhood?"

"Why is that, I wonder?"

"I don't know. But I think it's sad that when adults are irresponsible, children try and take on the adult responsibilities."

"It's weird. But I think that would pretty much describe a lot of my childhood." She looked at him in amazement. "What—

are you some sort of psychoanalyst, a mind reader, or something?"

He laughed. "No, but I like to study human nature. I think I'd have liked to have been a sociologist." Mertie plunked down two steaming bowls of chowder and a basket of bread, and Kestra realized how hungry she was. The chowder was thick and creamy, with large chunks of clams and an occasional grit of sand. They ate quietly for a while, but it was a comfortable silence, not really like that of two strangers.

"So Kestra, how did your grand opening go last month? The one you were so worried about?"

"Oh, that," she laid down her spoon and smiled. "It was a complete and total disaster."

"Really? What happened? I remember you mentioned something about some guy throwing a fit if you were late." He looked down at her hand, the one with her wedding ring still in place. "Would that be your husband?"

"No, that was my stepson, Greg—also half-owner of the restaurant. He'd already managed to turn the whole opening into something of a fiasco. I hate to imagine what his father would've thought if he'd been alive to see the circus." She took a bite of bread. "Oh, I'm sorry, Quin, I've never been one to tell a story in consecutive order.

"You see, my late husband, Jack McKenzie, started these restaurants about twenty years ago. He had a goal of offering the finest cuisine in the finest setting, and so on. There are four McKenzie's now, but he never wanted to expand too fast. He wanted each one to be special and to run with perfection." She glanced around the dingy chowder house. "Jack never would have darkened the door of a place like this. Not that I'm like that. Actually, aside from that silly memory, I find this place rather charming. But as far as McKenzie's goes, Greg and I haven't seen eye to eye about anything since his father died a couple years back, and consequently, I just sold out my share of the business to him. And do you know, for the first time in years I feel almost completely free. And it's super!"

"Well, I'm happy for you." She noticed the lines around his eyes deepen. "It sounds like you made the right choice to get out."

She nodded. "It wasn't easy, but now I'm glad."

He looked out over the ocean, and his eyes were a thousand miles away. She took the opportunity to admire his profile, deep set eyes, straight nose, firm mouth, all framed neatly by his dark beard. He looked like he could have been a sea captain on a clipper ship in days gone by. He turned and she pretended to be looking out the window as well.

"So now, Kestra, what do you plan on doing with all this new-found freedom?"

She remembered her bid on the house and felt like a little girl with a big exciting secret. She knew her whole face was smiling, but she just couldn't help it. "You won't believe what I've just done!"

"Try me." He was smiling, too, and to her, his face was like sunshine.

"Well, I just made an offer on *the house.*"

His brows lifted slightly. *"The house?"*

"Yes, you know—the estate on the bluff. Last month, after I'd been down here, I learned it was for sale. In fact, the idea of buying that house actually motivated me to sell out of McKenzie's. And that's why I came back. I want to renovate it and possibly turn it into a restaurant. After all, I did learn a thing or two about the business in the past few years."

His smile had vanished, and his face seemed to darken. Not in an angry way, more like when the clouds moved in and blocked the sun. She felt disappointed by this dismal reaction.

"Are you really sure about this, Kestra?" he asked. "I know

the place pretty well, and it'll require major work, not to mention money. It might be ages before it could realistically house a restaurant, and even then the return on your investment would take ages to occur, maybe not even within your lifetime."

She felt slightly indignant. She had thought he understood her. Why had he suddenly become so dense about this, especially when it was obviously so vital to her? "Quin, I'm not doing this to make money. I suppose, as far as a business decision, it may seem foolish. But there's a lot more to it than that."

"Such as?"

She longed for just a trace of that smile, some form of encouragement. But at least he seemed genuinely interested. Maybe, like Dan, he was concerned for her financial welfare. Actually, this was exactly the type of reaction she'd have gotten from Jack if he were still alive. Maybe it was just a man thing.

"For me, getting this house is partly about fulfilling a childhood dream. It will probably sound silly and sentimental to you, but as a young girl I used to look at that house and wish I lived there. It was like an old familiar friend to me, and even more than that, it was my personal symbol of hope. Somehow just seeing it reminded me there could be more to life. Anyway, more than the hand I'd been dealt. In fact, I even had a secret name for it."

"What was that?"

Mertie came and refilled their coffee mugs and picked up their empty bowls. Kestra poured in some cream and stirred, listening to the clinking of the spoon against the mug. Why was she telling him all this? He'd probably think she was some sort of nut case.

"I never told anyone before, but I call it The Wise Man's House." She studied his eyes for a reaction.

"After the man who built his house on a rock?" he asked.

She nodded.

61

"That's a perfect name." Yet, even as he smiled, his eyes looked sad. Or was it her imagination?

He glanced at his watch. "This time it looks like I'm the one who has to rush off. Kestra, I wish you the very best with your house." He reached over and touched her hand.

"Well, I don't really know if it's *my* house, not yet anyway."

"I suspect it is." He slowly removed his hand from hers, picked up the bill and stood. "Thanks so much for joining me today, Kestra."

"Thank you. And thanks for listening to my babbling." She wanted to say more. She wanted to ask if he'd be coming back this way again—or if he felt anything like she felt. But she could think of no sensible way of putting her feelings into words. Besides, it was like something had changed between them. Everything was going so well, and then some invisible barrier had sprung up when she began talking about the house. Maybe he was intimidated by the fact that she could afford to buy such an estate. After all, he'd only been leasing the caretaker's cottage. She had no idea what he did for a living. If he was an artist, as she'd suspected that first day, he might be struggling just to make ends meet.

The sun was already down as they walked across the gravel parking lot. When they reached her car, he momentarily grasped her hand again, then said good-bye. That was all—just good-bye.

She sat in her car a moment and watched the taillights of his Land Rover turn south and slowly disappear. His vehicle was not that of a starving artist. It was all so confusing. She slowly pulled out and turned north toward Port Star. She hadn't meant to, but she couldn't help stopping at the house. She parked in the drive without getting out and waited for her eyes to adjust.

Finally she could depict the black shape of the house against the evening sky. She sat there for a long time, trying to make sense of the afternoon's encounter. Would she ever see him again? Had she just imagined something special had happened between them? He really didn't say anything to encourage her or give her that hope. And their good-bye had seemed so final.

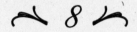

8

"Kestra McKenzie, where have you been?" demanded Holly before Kestra could even close the door behind her. "We were about to send out a search party!"

Matthew nudged Holly and added, "You're lucky, Kestra. As much as Dan and I tried to change her mind, Holly still refused to put the crabs in until you got here—the sign of a true friend."

Kestra made a graceful apology. It was a talent she'd mastered in the short time she'd been married to Jack—how to graciously say you're sorry, even if you aren't. In fact, she had stayed too long at the wonderful house. When she finally remembered Holly's dinner party, it was already too late to get back in time.

She went into Holly's bedroom and collapsed on the bed. There was a hard dry lump in her throat, but she was determined not to cry. What was there to cry about? She should be glad for an opportunity to spend a few hours with such an interesting man. A man whose mere existence had reminded her that such men really did exist! That in itself was worth quite a lot. And that should help her get through this dinner party.

She got up and pulled a light green sweater over her head,

then slipped on some earrings. Just as she began to untangle her hair, the phone rang. Knowing that Holly was busy getting dinner on the table, Kestra picked it up. For one crazy moment she thought it might be Quin, but in the same instant realized he wouldn't possibly know Holly's name or telephone number. She had to quit thinking like a high school girl.

"Hello," she answered in a flat tone.

"Hello, Kestra McKenzie? This is Jan."

"Yes?" Kestra sensed the eager note in Jan's otherwise strictly business voice.

"Kestra, I have good news about your offer."

"Did I get the house?"

"Exactly!"

Kestra jumped up and the phone clattered to the floor. She grabbed it and continued. "Are you still there, Jan? Oh, thanks so much! I really needed to hear this just now! Sure, I'll be by—first thing in the morning." She hung up and danced into the other room.

"I got it! I got it!" she yelled.

Holly dropped a big red crab back into the pot with a splat. "You mean the house? You got the house?" Kestra hugged Holly.

"Congratulations, Kestra," exclaimed Dan, patting her on the back and trying to sneak a hug. Kestra managed to avoid him as she shook hands with Matthew.

"Great going," said Matthew. "Now if you need any concrete, you just call, and I'll give you my special rate."

"All right, you guys, everything is ready, and now we've really got some serious celebrating to do," announced Holly as she laid the last dish on the table.

"Holly, everything looks scrumptious," exclaimed Kestra. "How did you know this was going to be a celebration dinner?"

"Just my feminine intuition, I guess."

"Do you cook like this all the time?" asked Dan.

Holly laughed. "Sure. Every night's a feast, right, Kestra?"

"Only if you count frozen dinners and hot dogs. But honestly, Holly has surprised me upon several occasions with her culinary skills."

"Well, I know I'm impressed," said Matthew with a big smile directed at Holly. Kestra was glad for her friend. She knew this was exactly the reaction Holly had hoped for.

Later Kestra helped Holly in the kitchen while the guys cleared the table.

"Kestra, do you think you and Dan could run out for ice cream, or maybe Matthew and I could?" whispered Holly.

"Uh-huh, I think I'm catching your drift." Kestra wasn't eager to spend time alone with Dan, but for Holly's sake she would.

"Hey, Dan," called Kestra. "It seems we have a dessert emergency on our hands. Holly made peach cobbler but forgot to get any ice cream."

"No problem," called Dan. "Care to join me, Kestra?"

Kestra forced a smile. "Sure, why not." She owed Holly one for being late.

Dan's big club-cab pickup was a mess, with various tools, old paper cups, and candy bar wrappers strewn about.

"Just give me a minute to straighten up this junk heap. I'm not used to taking ladies out." He scooped out all the stuff and heaved it back into his canopy. In spite of herself, she smiled. It was sort of sweet to see him grovel like this.

He held the door open for her. "Your chariot awaits, my lady."

Inside, the pickup smelled of sawdust and tools. It wasn't an unpleasant smell, just unusual. When she thought about it, Dan's whole way of life was foreign to her. And yet at one time, she'd have given anything to have been Mrs. Dan Hackett. Now the thought almost made her laugh.

"I think it's really great—your getting the house, I mean."

66

"Thanks. I can't wait to get started on it."

"Do you want me to come by and draw up a work plan for you to consider?"

"Huh?" Kestra wasn't really sure she wanted Dan to be this involved in her house. He'd had some good input, but how would it be to work with him on a daily basis? The idea alone made her nervous.

"Maybe you had some other contractor in mind..." His voice sounded like a sad little boy.

"No, it's not that. I haven't asked anyone else yet."

"I don't want to pressure you, Kestra. Just because we're old friends and all. But I am between jobs right now, and if you're interested I could start right away."

"Well, I don't know. Maybe you could come over and make out a work plan?"

"Sure thing, Kestra. I'll start on it, first thing next week. I've got a guy over in Polmo who knows a lot about this style of roof. I'll get him to come over and give me some tips. You can't get those shakes down here, but I know a place up in Washington that specializes in unusual roofing materials."

Kestra felt like she was being swept away with the tide. She hadn't actually agreed to let him do the work, had she? But Dan went on and on with what big plans he had for her house. She let him ramble, and she tried to listen, but instead she kept thinking about Quin. And the lump in her throat came back.

When they returned with the ice cream, Holly and Matthew were seated cozily before the little gas fireplace drinking coffee. They hadn't seemed to miss them a bit. Kestra and Dan went in and dished up the cobbler and ice cream. Kestra hoped everyone would eat fast and call it a night. She was tired. Tired of smiling and nodding, but mostly tired of Dan. Would this day never end?

She rinsed the last bowl and overheard Matthew announce

he had a working day tomorrow and better be heading off. Dan followed suit, and soon they were gone. Kestra kicked off her shoes and sank into the couch next to Holly.

"Ah, I thought they'd never leave," she sighed.

"Really? I was just wishing Matthew would have stayed longer." Holly sat down beside her. "He's so interesting. I feel like I've known him all my life, and at the same time, I hardly know him at all. Do you know what I mean?"

"Yes." Kestra knew, only too well. She thought about confiding to Holly about Quin. She tried to think of some way to bring it up casually, but before she knew it, Holly had taken off listing all of Matthew's wonderful attributes and personality traits. It was Kestra's turn to listen for a change. She owed Holly at least that much.

"Hey, earth to Kestra? You're not even here. You might as well go to bed, sleepyhead."

"Sorry, Holly. It has been a long day."

"Yeah, for me, too. Hey, congratulations again on your house. That should give you something good to dream about."

Kestra smiled. She hoped she'd dream about Quin. She wondered if it was possible to plant dream seeds in her mind before she went to sleep. Instead, she decided to pray. She'd put the whole matter of Quin into God's hands. After all, God had gotten her the Wise Man's House, and that had seemed an impossible dream at one time.

The next morning, Kestra met Jan at the escrow office. Kestra wanted to sign the papers on the house as soon as possible, so that everything would be pinned down, and no one could come in and take her house away. The stack of papers seemed endless, and midway through she wished she'd asked someone else to read them with her. But Jan and the escrow lady were patient, explaining the parts that were unclear. Kestra could hear Jack whispering to her that it was important to read every line. Finally, she signed her check, set down the pen, and sighed.

"Come on over to my office, and I'll give you the keys to your new house," said Jan.

"Great, I can't wait." Kestra walked with Jan down the street without speaking. The realty office was only two doors down.

"You know, you really were lucky on this house," said Jan in a conspiratorial manner as she handed over the keys.

"How's that?"

"Well, remember that other one who was interested?"

Kestra nodded—the man from California.

"Well, he'd made a full-offer bid that was naturally higher than yours. I thought for sure the house would be his when the owners agreed to sell. Then just last night, before I even had a chance to tell him the good news, he called me. And right out of the blue, he asked me to tear up his bid—just like that." Jan snapped her fingers.

"Really?" Kestra couldn't imagine how anyone could have backed out on the Wise Man's House.

~ 9 ~

W hat are you going to do with this old furniture, Kestra?"
asked Holly. She wiped her finger across the old pine
table, leaving a trail through the dust. Kestra had brought
Holly to the caretaker's cottage for some suggestions on how to
make the place more livable, and suddenly she felt unsure as to
whether she wanted to change anything. It was almost as if she
could still feel Quin's presence in the place. Did she want to
disturb that?

"We could always have a garage sale, or maybe just a big
bonfire," laughed Holly. "Of course, there might be a couple
things worth salvaging here, but that couch has definitely got to
go. On the other hand, this table has possibilities."

"Yes, I'd like to save the table." Kestra remembered that cold
February day when she and Quin had sipped coffee here.

"So, Kestra, what kind of look are we going for here? That
table definitely sets the tone for a more country or lodge-type
decor, but I'd always thought you were more the neo-classical,
traditional type."

"I'm not really sure, Holly. Jack was the one who made all
those decisions. I never had much of a chance to find out what

70

I really like. But I think for this cottage, something more casual would be fitting, don't you?"

"Exactly! I don't want to influence you. I want you to decide the direction you want to go, then I'll help get you there. That's how I work with people who come in for decorating advice in my shop. Then they can't come back and blame me if they don't like something because I just remind them they were the ones who picked it out."

"Smart businesswoman!" Kestra walked across the wood floor. It was definitely worn and even a little uneven. "I'd like to leave the floor basically as is, maybe find a couple of colorful area rugs."

"Hey, I just got a new carpet catalog at my shop. There's a really great-looking Navajo rug in reds and browns."

"Yes, something like that would be perfect! And then some of that wood-framed furniture with the big cushions—like that one in your shop."

"Sort of Mission Style?"

"I guess that's what you call it."

"Oh, this cottage is going to look fantastic, Kestra. What do you want to do with the kitchen floor? This old linoleum has got to go." Holly bent over and lifted a peeling corner. "Hey, there's wood under here. It could be sanded and sealed to match the rest."

"Great, and I think these cabinets just need a coat of paint. Maybe I could do that myself."

"Have you ever painted cabinets?"

"No, but there's a first time for everything. Besides, I don't really want to put a lot of money into this place—just make it livable, you know."

"Right. You'll have plenty to do in the big house. What about your furnishings back in Seattle. What do you plan to do with those?"

"I'm not sure. Some things will probably work okay in the 'big house' as you call it. But I'll probably need to get rid of some of the more modern stuff. You know, I never really liked the modern look. It was more Jack's thing."

"Well, next Saturday, Matthew and I could help you move these things out, and maybe we could rip up that floor or something."

"Oh, that'd be great, Holly. Matthew's so nice. You guys really seem to be coming along."

Holly smiled sheepishly. "I know. Actually it's kind of scary meeting someone like Matthew. He's so much like what I've always thought I wanted. It makes me sort of afraid."

"Why?"

"Oh, it's silly and paranoid. But it's—well, he's so perfect. I'm worried I might lose him and end up brokenhearted. Now isn't that dumb?"

Kestra thought about Quin. "No, I think I understand, Holly."

"Yes, I suppose you would. I guess you know what it's like to lose someone."

Kestra nodded. She knew Holly meant Jack, and that was fine. She wasn't ready to tell Holly about Quin. Sometimes she wondered if Quin might have been the product of her imagination anyway.

"Oh, Kestra, look at the time. I told Mom I'd be back by two. It's so sweet of her to watch the shop for me, I really don't like to be late. Of course, she loves doing it. It gives her a chance to get out and visit with folks. I'll see if she wants to take Saturday, too, so I can come help you. You picked a good time of year. Tourist season won't really begin until May. Hey, I'll bring home some catalogs tonight, and we can pick out some things for here."

"Thanks, Holly. Where would I be without you?"

"Probably richer. But not any happier!"

Kestra smiled as Holly pulled on her coat. "As usual, you're right, Holly. See you later."

Kestra stayed and puttered around. This was officially her property now, and she wanted to feel like she belonged here. But the cottage still felt like Quin's. Could he have been the one who made the other offer? As glad as she was to have the house, she wondered what it would be like if Quin were the owner now. She decided it was better not to think of that and started ripping off layers of shelf paper from the kitchen cabinets. Soon she found herself pulling off layers of wallpaper and everything was turning into a great big mess. Some layers of wallpaper felt like they were cemented to the wall, and she knew she'd better get some professional advice.

Kestra went back into the small bedroom and sat on the twin-sized bunk. The room was very spartan, with only the bed and a rickety chest of drawers. She ran her hand over the striped ticking mattress cover. Quin had slept here. The covering reminded her of the mattress she'd had as a child. In fact, her room had been very much like this—a bed, a dresser, a chair, and closet. Of course, her mother had tried to perk it up with odds and ends she'd pick up for half price at the drug store, usually chipped or shopworn, but Kestra had been glad to have them just the same.

In the narrow closet, a few wire hangers hung limply on the wooden rod. She reached up to peel the old shelf paper from the top shelf and as she pulled the curling, yellowed paper off, an envelope fell to the floor. Her heart raced as she read her own name written neatly across the top in clear blue ink.

She sat down on the bed and slowly opened the envelope. She knew it was from Quin.

Dear Kestra,

Congratulations, my friend! By now, you must be the new owner of the Wise Man's House. I'm sorry I had to run out on you so suddenly, but I had some urgent business to attend to, plus I was due back in San Francisco the next day. However, I know our meeting was not accidental, and I'd like to think we'll meet again. Although I can't say when, I do intend to return sometime to see how your renovation and restaurant project is doing. And for the record, I am glad this very special piece of property found its way into the hands of a wise woman.

Sincerely, Quin Larson

She reread it several times, then carefully refolded the note and placed it back in the envelope. She lay back on the bed and closed her eyes. So he didn't think their meeting was accidental. He planned to return. Was she crazy to be so happy? She asked God to help her get a better perspective. After all, she was the owner of The Wise Man's House, and she wanted to be, as Quin had said, a wise woman. She'd never considered herself to be very wise about anything, and usually when other people described her, they used words like impulsive, impetuous, even moody. More than anything she wished she could become wise, but she knew that real wisdom could only come from God. And she wasn't so sure that she was worthy. Just the same, she asked him to make her wise.

In the same moment, in another part of her mind, she silently pleaded for God to bring Quin back. But she wouldn't classify that as a prayer. No, surely that wouldn't be how a wise woman would pray.

H olly and Matthew met Kestra at the caretaker's cottage on Saturday as planned. To Kestra's dismay, Dan showed up shortly after they arrived.

"I hear you're gutting the place today, Kestra. Need an experienced hand?"

"Hi, Dan." She put more cheer in her voice than she felt. "No, we are not 'gutting the place.' We're just taking out some of the old furniture and removing this old floor covering, and whatever else we have time for."

"Well, here I am, at your service." He smiled, and it was impossible to turn him away. Besides, she told herself, it was free labor.

"Did you bring any tools?" asked Holly, the ever practical one.

"Did I bring tools?" Dan laughed. "Holly, Holly… Of course I brought tools."

"Well, come on in," exclaimed Matthew. "And grab the other end of this couch. Kestra wants all this stuff out to the stable for now."

"What's the thing with you and Dan, Kestra?" asked Holly as

soon as the fellows were out of earshot. "You get so cold and prickly whenever he's around. It just looks like he's trying to be nice."

"I don't know, Holly. He really irritates me. Maybe it's just unresolved differences."

"You mean with Melinda?"

"That's probably part of it, but there's more. I wish he'd give me some space. It seems like every time I turn around, there's Dan Hackett with a big grin, wanting to be a part of the action. I can almost see him wagging his tail, you know what I mean?"

Holly laughed. "Well, I should warn you. There's already been talk in town about you two getting back together."

The broad knife Kestra was using to scrape off wallpaper skidded off the wall and sliced into her left hand just below the thumb. She let out a loud yelp.

"Kestra, it's just idle gossip—you don't need to come unglued," replied Holly from her task. Kestra sank to the floor and stared at her gaping wound, then grabbed a rag to stop the blood.

"I cut myself, Holly. It doesn't look too good."

Holly's face turned white when she saw the blood-soaked rag dripping onto the floor. "Kestra, I'm not very good around blood." Holly leaned over and grabbed the counter, and Kestra knew she was not going to be much help. Just then the men came back. Dan instantly took over.

"Looks like it needs stitches, Kestra. Here, don't use this dirty rag." He grabbed a roll of paper towels and pressed it into her hand. "Hold this on tight, and I'll drive you over to the hospital to get you stitched up. Can't leave you females alone with real tools for a minute before you go off and do something like this."

"Very funny," said Holly as she sank limply into a chair.

"And you're not exactly Florence Nightingale, Holly," teased

Dan as he ushered Kestra out the door.

"Thanks, Dan," muttered Kestra. He practically picked her up and loaded her into his truck. She felt light-headed, and the paper towel roll was quickly getting soaked with her blood.

"Just lie down across the seat and keep pressing that tight, Kestra. It'll hold back the bleeding. It looks like you may have hit a vein."

She didn't really want to lie down, but he gently eased her over, and she was too weak to resist. He spoke soothingly as he drove, and he occasionally touched her head. This was a side of Dan Hackett she'd never seen.

The next thing she knew she was at the hospital, and a nice gray-haired doctor was bandaging her hand.

"Aren't you the O'Brian girl?"

"I used to be." She looked up at him. "Why, Dr. Mitchell, I guess I didn't recognize you."

"Well, I had the advantage. You weren't feeling too great when Dan brought you in. Besides that, I'd heard you were back in town. My wife's a regular customer at Holly's shop down at the Cannery. You managed to sever a small vein, young lady, but we stitched it all back up."

"Thanks. I guess I'm not too handy with tools yet."

He chuckled. "I hear you plan on renovating the old Murray Mansion. You don't intend on doing it all yourself, I hope."

"No, we were just working on the caretaker's cottage. I plan to live in it temporarily while the rest of the place is getting worked on."

"I always admired that old house. I hear you plan on turning it into a fancy restaurant."

"That's right. My late husband was a restaurateur, and I'd like to try my hand at it now."

"Well, just don't try this one." He held up her bandaged hand. "At least not for a while."

"Thanks, Dr. Mitchell."

"Sure thing, and good luck with your restaurant. I know my wife is looking forward to it." He winked.

She sat in the tiny cubicle for a few minutes while a nurse removed the instrument tray. Dr. Mitchell had been her mother's doctor. She appreciated that he hadn't mentioned the fact. Even back then, he'd seemed sensitive to her difficulty in dealing with things. And when her mother had died, he'd taken time to talk with and console her. He had genuinely seemed to care. He was a good man.

"So how's the patient doing?" asked Dan, poking his head in the door. "Ready to blow this joint?"

"Sure." She hopped down and was surprised that her knees wobbled beneath her. Dan grabbed her arm.

"Easy does it, gal. I think we should get some food and fluid into you. You lost a fair amount of blood, but fortunately they didn't need to transfuse any."

"Thanks, Dan. Maybe we could get pizza to take back to Matthew and Holly."

"Good idea, Kestra. But you always were the one to come up with the best ideas."

"Oh, you mean like buying old derelict houses?" She knew that was not what he meant. But just because he had taken her to the hospital, didn't mean she had to go down memory lane with him.

They picked up pizza and headed back. Kestra was careful to keep the conversation on safe ground. She wanted it to be perfectly clear that she wasn't inviting Dan Hackett back into her heart.

"Oh, Kestra, are you okay?" exploded Holly before Kestra even got in the door. "I was so worried, I thought you'd practically cut off your arm, but Matthew said it wasn't all that bad." She pulled out a chair. "Here, sit down."

"Relax, Holly, I'm fine. See," she held up her hand. She slowly looked around the cottage and tried to keep her face from showing what her heart felt. It seemed as if all traces of Quin had been erased.

"What's wrong? Didn't we get enough done?" asked Holly.

"No, you guys are amazing! You got all the linoleum off, and even sanded down the wood. And the wallpaper's gone! Wow, I guess I'll just have to get myself hauled off to the hospital every time I need some work done!"

Holly smiled proudly. Kestra knew it was probably for the best. She needed to forget about Quin. She was blowing him up too much in her mind. She needed to concentrate on the here and now.

"Fine. Just make sure you always come back with lots of food," exclaimed Matthew, as he ripped open the pizza boxes. "We're starved."

Finally they went back to work, but they hardly let Kestra help at all, and the pain medication the doctor had prescribed made her groggy.

"Holly, why don't you take Kestra home, and we'll work a little longer," suggested Matthew.

"Yeah, I was just thinking the same thing," agreed Holly. "Let's go, Kestra. You look beat."

Kestra wanted to argue but knew it was useless. They were right. She was only getting in the way.

"I was tired anyway," confided Holly as they headed toward the car. "But we made a pretty good dent on the place."

"You guys sure did. I wish I could have done more."

"That's okay. We expect to come out and have some really good times at your place for a repayment. Matthew and I have already been making plans for picnics and barbeques. It's a great place, Kestra, and it's exciting to get to share in it with you. Matthew and I took a break and walked around the big house a bit. It's the first time he's ever really seen it up close. He was pretty impressed. I was even thinking, once it's restored, it would make a terrific setting for a wedding."

"Yes, it would be nice for a wedding. Can you imagine coming down that staircase?"

Holly sighed. "It would be beautiful. Ha! Listen to us. Like a couple of dreamy school girls! Although I must say, it seems you've warmed up to Dan a bit. Did his chivalry pay off? He really came through by rescuing the maiden in distress."

"Well, it didn't hurt his case any. But honestly, Holly, I have no intention, whatsoever, of ever becoming romantically involved with Dan."

"The best laid plans of mice and—"

"I mean it, Holly. In fact—" Kestra cut herself short. She wasn't ready to disclose her feelings for Quin. It was all so unreal, not anything she could talk about without sounding like a sentimental idiot.

"In fact—what?"

"Oh, nothing…"

"Come on, you were about to say something, Kestra."

Kestra thought quickly. "In fact, I think Matthew is a much better catch than Dan."

"I couldn't agree with you more," gloated Holly.

"So see, if you keep pushing me towards romance, you better be careful. My eyes might wander over to Matthew."

"You wouldn't dare!"

"Of course not, silly, but just lay off on matching me up with Dan, okay? I don't mind his friendship, but that's all. Understand?"

"I guess so, but it's so much fun doing things with you as a foursome, you can't blame me for at least trying."

Kestra enjoyed the foursome, too. She just wished it could be with Quin instead of Dan. Then she wondered how Quin would fit into that group. He had seemed so serious, but then she really didn't know him that well. Maybe that was the point, she didn't know him. Perhaps she was just molding his character in her mind and falling in love with her creation. But then she remembered the golden flecks in his eyes, and the warmth of his hand on hers. That was not her imagination!

~ 11 ~

You were right about that lamp, Kestra," said Holly as she adjusted the alabaster shade. "It's perfect. See, you do have good taste."

"Maybe, but I wouldn't have pulled this together without you, Holly. I wish we'd taken before-and-after photos. This doesn't even look like the same place. The white walls make it seem so much larger, and it's certainly brighter—more cheery." She sat down on the new sofa and ran her fingers over the rich, dark woven upholstery. "And the colors in this fabric are perfect with that Navajo rug."

"Perhaps we should go into interior decorating. We make a pretty good team."

"I'll keep that in mind just in case the restaurant business doesn't pan out."

"When do your things come from Seattle?"

"Supposedly next Thursday. Why? Are you trying to get rid of me?"

"No, I'm not trying to get rid of you, I was just curious. To tell you the truth, I've gotten used to being roomies. I'm going to miss our late night popcorn parties."

"And I'll miss getting up to the smell of your fresh ground coffee. Of course, I won't miss the noise your coffee grinder makes."

"Well, it's better than an alarm clock."

"Maybe after I get all settled in, you could come out and spend the night once in a while, for old time's sake."

"Sure thing, and I'll even bring my coffee grinder."

Kestra smiled. Actually, she was more than ready to be back on her own again. Although she would definitely miss Holly's friendly chatter and positive outlook.

"It might be strange for you at first, being out here all alone. Do you think you'll get scared?"

"I don't know. I haven't given it much thought. But they just hooked up the phone. That will help."

"Maybe you should get a dog. Matthew was just telling me his brother has Irish Setter pups for sale."

"Holly, you're kidding! I love Irish Setters. I've never had a dog. I desperately wanted one in Seattle, but Jack didn't think it was right to keep a dog in the city. The lady next door had a Scotty, and he always seemed perfectly happy to live in the city. She took him to the park every day, and he wore little coats and things. Actually I think he thought he was a human. She wanted to help me find a Scotty, too, but Jack said no. He thought it would mess up the condo. I suppose I could have gotten one after Jack died, but it still felt like it was his home, not mine."

"Well, I suppose Jack was right. Dogs can be hard on a place, especially big ones like Irish Setters." Holly looked around at Kestra's new furnishings.

"But a dog would have lots of room to run and play here. Just think of romping on the beach. Oh, yes, Holly, I want one of those pups! Can we call Matthew?"

"I'm going out with Matthew tonight. Maybe he can arrange

for you to see the pups. But you should give this some thought, Kestra."

"I have. And I want a dog. That's all there is to it."

"Yes, I can just see you with an Irish Setter. It would go with your hair, not to mention your Irish temperament. It sounds perfect. Are you ready to go now? I told Matthew I'd go with him to the movies at seven."

"You know, Holly, I almost feel like spending the night here tonight. It's so cozy now, with all the furniture in place. And I'd like to make a fire in the fireplace. Besides, you're going to be out most of the evening."

"I don't blame you, Kestra. This place is so cute, it makes me want to move in, too. But don't worry, I need to stay close to my shop, so I won't be joining you. Where will you sleep until your bed comes?"

Kestra patted the sofa. "This feels pretty comfortable."

"Well, let's get going, you can pick up some bedding and things at the apartment."

It was dark when Kestra returned to the cottage, and she'd forgotten to leave a light on. She carried her first load to the cottage, pausing on the walkway. She hadn't been there at night for some time, but the sound of the ocean was comforting, and even in the darkness the place had a friendly, homey feel.

It took three trips to bring in all the stuff Holly had insisted she take until her own things came. But each time she walked up to the cottage and saw the golden light streaming from the windows, she felt like a fairy tale character coming home to the little cottage in the woods, after having been lost for a long time.

She sat the last box inside the door and looked around the cheerful room with approval. She wondered what Quin would think if he ever saw the place again. She had not liked erasing the way she remembered it when he lived here, but she knew it was for the best. It was her place now.

She used the wood scraps Dan had brought from a remodel job to build a fire in the small rock fireplace, and soon it crackled against the backdrop of the sound of the ocean. Someone had told her that once she lived by the sea for a while, she'd no longer hear the ocean. She hoped they were wrong. She loved that sound.

She carefully put away the food items, a small frying pan, a coffeepot, a couple of plates, and a few pieces of silverware. For the first time, she looked forward to her own things coming from storage in Seattle. She'd be happy to see her espresso machine, as well as a few other luxuries. Of course, she'd have to decide what to do with the rest of her stuff. But there was plenty of storage room in the carriage house and stable, and even in the attic once the roofing was complete.

She'd allowed Dan to start work on the roof of the big house. He'd been eager and willing, and she didn't have the heart to ask another contractor to make a bid. She didn't actually have a written bid from Dan, but he'd given her an estimate and they'd shaken hands, and he'd guaranteed her the best deal in town. Besides, since the day she'd cut her hand, Dan had seemed different to her. He was less pushy and more polite. Or maybe she just looked at him differently. Anyway, it was easier to be nice to him when he wasn't coming on to her.

She put the few personal items she'd brought in the tiny bathroom. Why hadn't she brought all her stuff from Holly's? This was it, she knew it now. She was moving in for good. Holly would understand. She could sleep on the couch until her bed came. Or maybe she'd buy a new bed. She didn't see how that big king-sized bed would fit in that small room anyway, but Holly had said it would. She emptied the last box, and there was the note. She'd tucked it in, planning to reread it. It was a luxury she'd allowed herself only twice since the day she'd found it in the closet. Each time she told herself that was the last.

She took a nice long shower, admiring the embossed tiles and old-fashioned brass fixtures she'd found in a renovation catalog. She'd decided the cottage was sort of a testing ground for what would come later in the big house. She'd hoped she could get by without having to hire a decorator, and so far everyone seemed to agree she and Holly had done a great job. It made her feel good to think she could make those kinds of decisions. She knew Jack hadn't meant to, but he'd always made her feel insecure about her own taste, because he was so sure of his own.

She and Holly had wallpapered the bathroom themselves, and done a very decent job, she thought as she dried herself. Holly had discouraged Kestra from choosing the plaid wallpaper, but Kestra had held firm. In the end, Holly agreed it was perfect, even if it was a pain to hang. Kestra wiped a circle on the steamy oak-framed mirror and realized she'd forgotten her hair dryer.

She made a cup of instant cocoa and sat by the fire to dry her hair. She was home. She didn't remember ever feeling so much at home—anywhere. Maybe she wouldn't move into the big house after all. This place really seemed like her own. After Jack had died, the lawyer told her the condo was in her name, but it had never felt like hers. She hadn't wanted to change anything because it was Jack's, and for all that time it was like a memorial to him. But this was hers.

She opened the note. She almost knew it by heart, but it still thrilled her to slowly read the words, to study the strong, even handwriting. It looked as if he'd used a fountain pen. Before she finished the last line, a noise outside startled her. It wasn't loud, but she knew she'd heard something. For the first time, she realized she had no coverings over the big front window. Holly had ordered some wooden shutters, but they hadn't come in yet. Kestra wished she'd thought to hang a sheet over the window. Maybe the noise was just a possum or something.

She remained next to the fireplace, afraid to move. She knew it was silly. If anyone was really out there, she was in plain sight, like a fishbowl. Not moving made no difference. She stared hard at the window, but could only see the reflection of the cottage's interior, and then blackness beyond. Someone could be standing there right now, staring at her. Somehow she felt certain someone was doing just that. It took every ounce of courage, but she forced herself to stand up and walk across the room to the phone, pulling her robe more tightly around her as she went. It seemed to take forever.

Just as her hand reached the phone, someone knocked loudly on the door, and she felt her heart stop.

"Hey, Kestra, are you home?"

It was Dan. For the first time in ages she was actually relieved to hear his voice. She ran over and threw open the door.

"Hi, Kestra. I heard you'd moved in and I brought you a house-warming present." He handed her a basket containing a bag of ground coffee, some fruit, and pastries.

"How thoughtful." She placed the basket on the counter. "But did you know you just about scared the daylights out of me?"

"I'm sorry, Kestra. I saw Matthew and Holly at the movies, and they told me you were out here all by yourself, and I wanted to drop by and make sure everything was okay." He walked over to the fire to warm his hands, then stooped over to pick up her letter from the floor.

"Aha, caught you reading old love letters—"

She snatched it. "No, it's not a love letter. I was just cleaning some things out of my purse." She lightly tossed the note and envelope into the fire and watched them curl and turn blue with flame. Finally the paper turned to black ash, and she felt like her heart was there with it. She tried to conceal her remorse and wondered why she'd done such a foolish thing. So what if she was reading what she wished were a love letter. What business was that of Dan?

"Say Kestra, how about I make you some of this coffee. It's some new kind of chocolate-almond flavor, and I had to smell it all the way over. I don't usually go for that gourmet stuff, but now I'm craving a cup." He was already in the kitchen filling the pot with water. "Your place looks great, Kestra. Really nice. You and Holly did a good job picking out all the furnishings and stuff. Although I'm a bit surprised. I thought you'd be more the type to go for frills and those pinky kind of colors. That's what Melinda always liked."

It was the first time he'd mentioned Melinda. She turned from the fireplace and studied him as he carefully measured the fresh-ground coffee into Holly's old coffeemaker. It wasn't really his fault she'd burned the note.

"You get the coffee going, and I'll go put on something more decent."

"You look pretty decent to me."

"One more comment like that and I'm throwing you out."

He held up his hands, "Just kidding, Kestra. Don't go get the gun."

She went into the bedroom and jerked on her jeans. Even though she was angry at him for interrupting her quiet evening and angry at herself for burning Quin's letter, she had to admit she was glad to have Dan here. That feeling of sheer fright hadn't left her yet. And she was thankful for any company, even if it was his.

"Here, help me put this sheet over the window. I forgot I was sitting in a fishbowl in here."

"Yeah, you can see right in. Not very smart for a woman

alone. You're pretty brave to stay out here by yourself, Kestra. Melinda couldn't stand being left alone, even though we lived in a nice quiet neighborhood."

That was the second time she'd ever heard him mention Melinda, and all in one night. She wondered if he wanted to talk about his marriage. The sheet securely in place, he poured coffee into two of Holly's mismatched mugs.

"Here's to your new home, Kestra. May it be a happy one," he clicked his mug to hers. "I almost brought over something more festive, but I figured you'd get the wrong idea and throw me out on my ear."

"Well, maybe you're starting to understand me after all, Dan."

"Yeah, well, I'm not quite the Neanderthal you take me for. I can take a hint. It's just that I'm persistent. And you know what they say, persistence pays off."

"Okay, now I'm thinking about throwing you out." She frowned at him. "Come on, Dan. Get a clue. I am only interested in you for two things: one, your professional skills; and two—" she hesitated. She didn't want to send the wrong signal. "Your friendship, and I mean just friendship. Nothing more. Do you understand?"

He nodded, looking like a kicked pup.

"Dan, don't you think we could be just friends? Or does it have to be something more for you? If that's the case, you may as well lay your cards on the table. Because friendship is all I'm offering."

"Actually, I could use a friend, Kestra."

"And you do understand the meaning of the word 'friend'?"

He grinned sheepishly. "So what are you saying? Do I need to sign something in blood here in order to be your friend?"

"I'll take you at your word, Dan. Just don't let me down."

⌁ 12 ⌁

Kestra collapsed on the couch. "I had no idea storing furniture would be such a chore, Holly. Thanks for all the help."

"I didn't realize you had so much stuff, Kestra."

"I didn't either. But I must admit it was fun to see the moving men pull more and more things out of those trucks. I never dreamed Jack had squirreled away so many treasures."

"Yeah, it was almost like Christmas. You know, Kestra—" Holly paused. "It was almost as if Jack knew..."

"I know, the same thought crossed my mind. So many of the pieces are just perfect."

"I think I have goose-bumps."

"Me, too." Kestra shivered. "My mom used to call things like this 'uncanny.' I always thought that was an odd word, but that's what I kept thinking. This was uncanny."

"But a good kind of uncanny."

"You know, Holly, this is one of those moments in my life when I just know for certain that I'm in God's hands. There have been so many times when everything seemed absolutely hopeless, when there seemed to be no rhyme or reason for why things happened like they did. But I need to remember times like right now."

"Yeah," Holly sighed. "I still can't believe you didn't know Jack had all those antiques in storage. Kestra, they must be worth a fortune."

Kestra nodded. "But it's not the monetary value that's so astounding. The weird part is how well they go with the house, as if they were picked out specially. That cherry bedroom set is perfect for the room I decided to use as my own. That is if I ever move in. I'm getting pretty attached to this little cottage."

"That's understandable right now. But wait until the big house starts looking this good. What did you think of all those dining room tables and chairs?"

"Jack must have been collecting with another restaurant in mind. Although it's odd because McKenzies always had matching dining room furnishings. The weird thing is that I had envisioned The Wise Man's House with different sets of antique tables and chairs, just like the ones that came out of those trucks today."

"Well, Kestra, I think you're right. God is watching out for you. Without a doubt. But unfortunately, it looks like you'll still be sleeping on the couch for a while. I could have sworn a king-sized bed would fit in that room. Well actually, it would have fit in the room, if they could have gotten it in the door."

Kestra laughed. "I don't care. I think I want to sell that bed now anyway." She felt an unexpected twinge of grief. She remembered the comfort she'd gotten from sleeping in Jack's bed after his death. It had made him seem nearby somehow.

"Is it sad? I mean seeing all those things again—and thinking of Jack?"

"Sort of. I thought I was past the sadness now. I've been so much happier back here. But I suppose it never really goes away—not totally."

"I guess not." Holly walked into the kitchen. "Do you want me to make us some tea?"

"That's a good idea, Holly. I made some gingersnaps yesterday. They're pretty hard, but they might be good with tea."

"Before you get too far along with your restaurant plans, you should think about finding a good chef." Holly filled the kettle and rinsed out the teapot. "Frankly, I don't think anyone would drive out here just to sample your culinary skills."

"Thanks a lot. For your information, I have no intention of cooking for the restaurant." Kestra laid the cookies out on a plate, and in no time the kettle was whistling.

They sat down at the pine table, and Holly shook her head as she poured tea. "I still can't believe it, Kestra. All those beautiful antiques and you knew nothing about them?"

Kestra dipped a cookie in her tea. "I remember shopping for antiques with Jack, but it was always just for fun. Although, come to think of it, he usually bought things. Usually the pieces needed work or refinishing, and he'd have them sent to storage. I guess I thought he was just reselling them or using them in the restaurants. I had no idea."

"I can't wait until the big house is ready. I want to see everything in place. It's going to be so beautiful, Kestra. And now you can concentrate on things like paint colors, wallpaper, lighting, and whatever."

"Yes, and you still promise to help me?"

"You think I would pass up a chance like this? It's like being a little girl with a giant doll house. Hey, I got a new catalog today with some really great-looking turn-of-the-century prints."

"Did you notice how the roof is coming?"

"Yeah, it looks like Dan's doing a terrific job. But where was the crew today? I didn't see any of them."

"I told him not to come out since the movers would be here, and he had another job to finish up anyway. Then he promised he and his guys will work out here exclusively until it's done."

"You are going to be one busy gal, Kestra. Speaking of busy, I need to scoot. I started a new girl this week at the shop, but this is her first day alone. She seems to be doing okay, but I need to help her close."

"Well, I really do appreciate your help out here today, Holly. Say, do you and Matthew want to come out here Friday night for dinner?"

"Sure, but should we eat first?" Holly clunked a gingersnap against the table.

"Very amusing. Actually, you might be surprised to find out there are a couple of things I can cook. Even if I'm not quite as adept as you."

"Okay, Kestra. But call me if you want me to bring pizza."

Kestra smiled. Holly didn't know everything about her. She would surprise them on Friday night with homemade pasta and clam sauce. That was one dish she made that even Jack had approved. Jack, dear sweet Jack. This delivery today was almost like a message from him. A confirmation that she was indeed doing the right thing. Even though he'd been such a perfectionist in his lifetime, he'd always believed in her, too. He'd always told her she could do anything she put her mind to. But she'd never really put her mind to anything before. It was always Jack who seemed to have the Midas touch. He was so successful, so well thought of, and liked, she had felt like a shadow next to him.

She went back out to the carriage house to check out some antiques again while it was still light enough to see. The wind was blowing and the fog was rolling in. She'd missed her daily walk on the beach, but helping find places for all the furniture had been a hearty work-out in itself. In the afternoon light she walked down one of the narrow paths they'd left between the many furnishings. She ran her hand across the top of a pine dresser. It was a primitive style and didn't really look like it belonged in the big house, but it would be perfect for storing her clothes in the cottage. She found several other pieces she wanted to move into the cottage, including an iron bed frame she hadn't noticed earlier. With a fresh coat of paint and a mattress, it would be just right for her bedroom. She heard gravel crunch in the driveway and poked her head out to see Dan's pickup parking in front of the cottage. She considered hiding out from him in the carriage house, but then realized he'd probably be willing to help her move some of this stuff.

"I'm out here," she called as he knocked on the cottage door.

"Hey, whatcha up to?" He walked over toward her. She could tell by his nice shirt and cowboy boots that he'd cleaned up from work. She, on the other hand, was a dusty mess, with a bandanna still tied around her hair. But she didn't care. After all it was only Dan.

"Come see my treasures, Dan."

He grinned. "I was about to show you a treasure myself."

"Huh?" What was he up to?

"But I'll look at yours first. What've you got here?"

She proudly threw open both doors of the carriage house.

He had a puzzled expression. "You getting ready to have a garage sale?"

"Not hardly! These are valuable antiques, Dan. They'll be the furnishings for the restaurant and the rest of my house. Aren't they wonderful?"

"Uh, yeah, sure. They just look so old and run-down."

"Dan Hackett, you are hopeless!"

"Well, excuse me if I don't like antiques as much as you do. It just looks like a bunch of old junk to me. My dad has a pile of stuff like this up in his attic. It doesn't seem like anything to get all excited over."

She shook her head. "Well, as long as you're here, how

about helping me move some of this old junk up to the cottage?"

"You want to put this stuff in your nice cottage? You got it all spiffed up in there, Kestra. Why do you want to clutter it up with this?"

"Dan, I'm not asking for your decorating expertise, just your muscle. Are you willing or not?"

He folded his arms across his chest. "Hmmm. How about we make a deal. I'll help you move the stuff, if you go out to dinner with me tonight."

"Dan, that's not fair. Remember what I said about being friends?"

"Look, I'm not asking you to go steady. Just dinner. You know, two friends going to dinner. I suppose you can't eat dinner with a friend?"

Kestra stared at him for a moment. Did he understand what she meant?

"Okay, Dan. I'll go with you as a friend. Nothing more. Now roll up your sleeves."

Finally the last piece had been put in place, and Kestra started rubbing lemon oil onto the top of the pine dresser. The grain seemed to come alive and glow with the rich warmth of old wood.

"You know, Kestra, this stuff doesn't look half bad in here after all." Dan nodded with approval.

"See, you could learn something new every day if you gave it a chance." Kestra caught a glimpse of herself in the old mirror propped against the wall, and cringed. "Oh, Dan, I'm not fit to go to dinner. Just look at me."

"I can wait while you clean up. Oh, yeah, I almost forgot. I have a surprise for you. You spruce up and I'll go get it."

As much as she'd have liked, she knew it would be rotten of her to back out now, after he'd been such a good sport. Oh, well, as Dan said, it was only dinner. She did a quick clean up and changed into fresh jeans. She was about to pull on her fisherman-knit sweater but opted for her dark-green silk blouse instead. She could, at least, try to look nice.

She stepped out, and there sitting in the middle of her floor was Dan with a copper-colored pup in his lap. The pup wore a lopsided blue bow and looked like it could hardly sit still.

"He's for you, Kestra. Matthew told me you were wanting an Irish Setter. And, well, here he is."

Kestra was speechless. The pup was beautiful and exactly what she'd hoped for. But she had wanted to pick it out herself. She didn't want it to be a gift from Dan. Was she just being petty? She looked at Dan, but saw no sign of malice. Instead he was grinning from ear to ear. It was awfully nice of him. Maybe she should just accept the gift. Why was it so hard?

"What's the matter? Say something, Kestra. Don't you like him?"

She knelt down, and the pup bounced right over to her, flopped his paws onto her knees, and gazed up at her with warm golden brown eyes. She stroked his coat. It was softer than silk. Those eyes—they reminded her of Quin's.

"Of course I like him, Dan. It's just—I was going to get him myself." She gently rubbed the pup behind his ears, and he licked her hand. "I didn't want someone else to get him for me. Not that I knew it was him," she pointed to the dog. "I mean any Irish Setter pup."

"So you don't like him?"

"No, I like him. I said that already. Don't you understand? I swear, sometimes you can be so thick, Dan Hackett!"

He laughed. "Now you sound exactly like the old Kestra I used to know."

"What do you mean?"

"Oh, I don't know. Something about you just now, reminded me of us—back in high school, I mean."

"Dan, we're not in high school, and I am not still sweet on you. Can't you get that through your head?"

"Yeah, I know. But just for the record, you were once—weren't you? Sometimes I think I imagined it all, Kestra. You can be so cold sometimes."

"Dan, you're impossible. Okay, just for the record, yes, there was one time in my immature, teenaged life when I thought the sun rose and set with you. But that was long ago. I was a different person back then, and so were you. Are you satisfied now?"

He looked down at his hands without saying anything. She wanted this moment to pass. They had never really discussed this subject, and she didn't feel ready to now.

"I know…I guess sometimes I just wish we could go back, Kestra."

"We can't, Dan. In fact, I wouldn't want to, even if we could."

"Sometimes I think you hate me, Kestra."

"Dan, why are you doing this? You know I don't hate you. Why would I agree to go to dinner with you if I hated you?"

"Because I twisted your arm."

"Okay, Dan. Why don't we just get this out in the open, once and for all. We had something going in high school, but if you will try to remember, we started to disagree a lot, we were fighting all the time. Then finally we broke up. I have to admit, I thought it was a temporary breakup. The next thing I knew you were engaged to Melinda. What was I supposed to think?"

"I don't know. I guess that I was a rotten bum."

"Well, that's just about right."

"I wanted you to come talk to me."

"Talk to you? About what? Was I supposed to come and say congratulations on your engagement, Dan, I'm so happy for you? For Pete's sake, you were barely twenty, and Melinda was nineteen. You'd always told me you weren't getting married until you were twenty-five. And I certainly didn't want to get married that young. It just made absolutely no sense."

"You mean other than the fact that Melinda was pregnant, supposedly with my baby. And my parents threatened to disown me if I didn't do the right thing."

Kestra was stunned. Melinda had been pregnant.

"Don't act so surprised, Kestra, everyone in town suspected."

"But there was no baby—"

"She miscarried right after we got married."

"I didn't know…"

"We tried to keep it a secret."

"But you stayed married."

"Yeah, it seemed like the right thing to do. Melinda was okay for the first couple years. It was sort of nice to come home to a clean house and dinner on the stove. And when Amber came along, it was pretty cool being a dad. But Melinda started to be such a nag about everything. She wanted me to help out with the baby and stay home all the time. I still liked doing stuff with my buddies, and she hated that. Pretty soon we were fighting like cats and dogs. She even turned Amber against me. Next thing I knew, I started hearing rumors about her and the tennis teacher at the Country Club. That's when I knew it was over."

"What about Amber? Isn't she about eight?"

"Yeah, poor kid. She thinks I'm the bad guy. Maybe someday she'll figure it out."

There was silence. Kestra didn't know what to say. She pretended to be focused on the pup as he chewed playfully on her fingers.

"So anyway, there you have it. The true story of Dan Hackett's messed up life. You know what this means, Kestra?"

"What?"

"Now you'll have to tell me about your marriage to your

restaurant tycoon. The true story. Friend to friend."

"All right, but not right now. I'm starting to get hungry."

"Okay, back to the dog. Do you want him or not?"

It was too late. The puppy had won her heart. There might be others out there, but this was the one she wanted. It was a dirty trick on Dan's part.

"Yes," she answered, humbled. "I want this pup. But only on one condition."

"Oh, so now you're the one making the deals. Okay, what is it?" He was grinning like he'd won the first round.

"You have to swear that there will be absolutely no strings attached to this gift. If I accept him, then this is my dog. You can't come over and act like we have joint custody or something. Otherwise you can take him right back."

"You really don't trust me, do you, Kestra."

His hang-dog look left her speechless, and she felt like an ogre. Here he'd just poured out his heart to her and was giving her a wonderful gift, and she was treating him like dirt. What was wrong with her?

"Dan, it's not a matter of not trusting you," she began slowly, groping for the right words. "It's just that I need some space. I keep feeling like you're pressuring me for something I can't give you."

He smiled. "Well, then I agree—absolutely no strings attached. This dog is a gift. He's yours totally. No joint custody. Now do you want me to write it in blood?"

"No, Dan, that won't be necessary."

"That's good, because YOUR dog just had an accident, right over there by the door."

~ 13 ~

Kestra dusted the books off and carefully placed them on the bookshelf. It was fun unpacking her things, many she had not seen for some time. The books, in particular, were like old friends.

"You're going to have to name him some time, Kestra," said Holly from the little kitchen. "You can't just keep calling him pup, or hey you. Come on let's think of some names." She flipped down a sliver of roast beef, and the pup gobbled it up. "How about Greedy. This dog is always begging. Don't you ever feed him?"

"Does he look starved to you?"

Holly laughed. "No, he looks pretty healthy."

"I've got it!"

"Got what?"

"I'll name him after my favorite author, Patrick O'Riley—he was even Irish, too."

"Oh, sure, I can just hear you calling. 'Here, Patrick O'Riley, come and get your dog chow.'"

"No, I'll just call him Riley for short."

"Hmm, now that's cute. Riley!" Holly tried it out. "Hey, he

likes it! Did you see his ears perk up?"

"Sure he likes it. Come here, Riley. That's a good boy." Kestra scratched him behind the ears. "See, this is a book by the man you're named after." She held up a book for Riley to see.

"Next thing, I suppose you'll be teaching him to read," laughed Holly. "Who is this Patrick O'Riley anyway? And will he mind having a dog named after him, even if it is an Irish Setter?"

"The guy's not around to care. He was an old Irish author who was popular around the turn of the century. He wrote tales about people in Ireland with a Christian message woven in. His grandson recently pulled them out of mothballs and is reviving them into modern language."

"Oh, I think I have heard of them. Maybe I could borrow one and try it out."

"Sure, but I have to warn you they're addictive. I can hardly wait for the next one to come out. About every six months a new one is released. I heard there's about twenty altogether, and I already have sixteen. It will be so sad when there aren't any more to look forward to."

"You could always start reading them over again. Sometimes I like to read a good book twice."

"That's an idea. Okay, how about I give you a hand with those sandwiches now. Before the work crew comes and storms our doors."

Together, Kestra and Holly carried the basket of food and a cooler of drinks over to the big house.

"This is really nice of you to feed these guys, Kestra. But really, I don't see why you do it. I mean, you're paying them good money to work here. It's not like you owe them any favors."

"I know. I only do it about once or twice a week. I want to keep them on my good side, and besides, Dan is giving me a good deal."

"Hey, here they come," called Dan. He came down from a

ladder. "How do you like that copper flashing, Kestra?"

"It looks great, Dan. And the roof is beautiful. Look how nice those shakes look in the sunlight."

"Yeah, and I've got my guys working in the third story right now, patching up where the roof leaked. What do you think you'll do with that huge room, Kestra? Have ballroom dancing?" He chuckled.

"You know, Dan, that's not a bad idea."

He groaned. "What you really should do is put a bar up there, with a couple of pool tables and a big-screened TV. That would really bring in some business."

"That's not the kind of business I'm looking for."

Dan bent over and patted Riley. "How you doing there, bud?"

"He has a name now. It's Riley."

"Riley. That's a pretty good name."

"We'll leave this lunch with you. Holly's here to help me pick out some wallpaper and paint colors for the upstairs. Do you still think it will be ready by May? I have a painter lined up, and I need to confirm it with him."

"Looks like we're right on target. Got the plumbers coming next week, and the electrician's supposed to come by today."

"Great—"

"Anyone here by the name of Kestra McKenzie?"

They turned to see a mailman pulling into the driveway.

"I'm Kestra."

"Well, a couple weeks ago I put a letter in your box, and there hasn't been another one until today. But I see this old one is still here. I thought I better bring them both up to you."

"That's odd. I have a box in town. All my mail goes there."

"Apparently not all your mail." He handed her the two letters. "Maybe you'll want to check it from time to time." He tipped his hat and smiled.

Her heart started to beat faster as she read the return address. They were from Quin.

"Who sent them, Kestra?" asked Holly.

"Oh, nobody. Let's go up and look at the second floor. We need to decide on those colors." She threw Holly a look that said 'later,' and stuffed the letters into the pocket of her denim jacket. She was dying to open them, but more than that she wanted to read them alone. Once upstairs, Holly started pestering her about the letters.

"Holly, I promise, I'll tell you all about it after I've had a chance to read them, okay?"

"All right. But I won't forget. I can tell by the look on your face it's something important, something you wouldn't want to keep from your best friend."

"You're right. I have been meaning to tell you. But I just wasn't sure there was anything to tell. It's a guy, okay? And I didn't know if I had simply imagined we had something going or if there really was something going. Do you understand?"

"Yes, it's about as clear as mud. So maybe we should just get these colors picked out so you can go read your letters in private." She jabbed Kestra with her elbow.

It was amazing how quickly they picked out the wallpaper and paint. Kestra wondered if all the decisions would be this easy. She had picked a simple striped wallpaper with a delicate vine threaded through for her bedroom. The accent paint would be ivory and the woodwork would remain the same dark cherry color to go with the bedroom set. Kestra could just imagine the tall four-poster bed in the high-ceilinged room.

"You know, Holly, once this place is ready, I may want to move in after all. The bathroom up here is bigger than my whole bedroom in the cottage. And I'm going to have Dan take those two closets and join them into one big walk-in closet. I know that's probably not historically correct, but it sure will be nice."

"You're lucky no one decided to list this house on the historic register. Then you'd have to jump through all kinds of hoops while you renovated."

"I know. I like the idea of keeping the place as authentic as possible, but I want it to be practical, too. Like the kitchen needs all kinds of modernization, but I don't want it to look all high tech."

"Yes, I saw an article in a design magazine where they refurbished an old English kitchen, but kept it looking like it was still in the last century. I'll show it to you later. After you've had a chance to read those letters. I can tell they're burning a hole in your pocket. See the smoke?"

Kestra smiled sheepishly, as she removed her hand from the pocket that held the letters.

"Kestra, why don't you take off and read them now. I can measure this room for the paper. And I'll start looking through these wallpaper books and see if I can find a good companion print for your bath. Maybe I can scout out a few for you to choose from."

"Really? That would be great. I won't take long."

"Sure, and then you can tell me what this is all about, like you promised."

"Okay, but we might have to go where there aren't so many listening ears about."

Kestra wanted to go back to the cottage, but the guys were still eating in the front, so she slipped out the back with Riley at her side and walked down the stone stairs to the beach. It was still sunny, and the breeze was barely blowing. She walked a short distance until she found her favorite piece of driftwood. She sat down on the dry sand and leaned against the smooth log, taking a deep breath. Two letters. Now, if there had been just one, she would have thought it was just a note congratulating her on the house or something insignificant. But two gave her hope. She studied the handwriting on the envelope, same crisp, clean writing as the note she had so foolishly burned that night.

She carefully opened and slowly read the first.

Dear Kestra,

I hope this finds you well and perhaps settling into The Wise Man's House. I suppose some of the rooms may be habitable, although I know you'll have much work ahead. The reason I'm writing is to inquire whether you might be interested in renting the caretaker's cottage to me. I've missed it and would like to be able to use it from time to time. Of course, you may have other plans for it, but I thought I would ask. It would also give me great pleasure to see you once again, Kestra. Although we spent so little time together, I feel I already know you well, and I would like the opportunity to get to know you even more. Once in a great while you meet someone, and it's as if you've always known them. That is how I felt when I met you, Kestra. I hope you won't think I'm presumptuous in writing like this, but I suspect you'll understand. If you care to rent out the cottage, please contact me at the address below. I'll only be there for a couple more weeks. After that, I'll need a place to stay for a while to complete a project I am working on. I hope that can be the cottage next to The Wise Man's House.

Sincerely, Quin.

She couldn't believe it, he was coming back. And not just for the scenery. He wanted to see her as well. Quickly she tore into the second letter. He'd said in two weeks, perhaps this letter was announcing he was on his way. He could even be arriving today.

Dear Kestra,

I've looked in vain for an answer to the letter I sent you a couple of weeks ago. I can only think I must have completely overwhelmed you with my forwardness. I'm truly sorry. You must think I'm very strange. I suppose in many ways I am. Please forgive me, Kestra. I've made other arrangements for my lodging. I'm sorry to have troubled you like this. Perhaps our paths will cross again someday.

Sincerely, Quin.

"No—No!" she cried. Riley jumped up in alarm, his tail wagging eagerly. "No, it can't be!" She searched the second envelope for a return address, but only his name was neatly printed across the top. Oh, why hadn't she thought to check that old rusty mailbox on the side of the road. Or why hadn't that foolish old mailman simply carried that first letter to her? Why, she asked herself, again and again, why? Maybe if she wrote back to the first address, the letter might be forwarded. But by now, Quin may have already settled someplace else.

She trudged slowly back up to the house. She knew Holly would be waiting. She had hoped to share good news. Now she just hoped she could hold back the tears.

Holly was seated on the bathroom floor surrounded by several opened wallpaper books. She looked up and frowned. "Hey, what's wrong, Kestra?"

"Oh, just some really bad timing."

"What do you mean?"

Kestra poured out the story, starting in the middle and working both ways simultaneously. Holly asked some questions for clarification, and Kestra realized how badly she'd muddled the details.

"No, Holly, he didn't own the house. He rented the cottage, but I think he tried to buy the house at the same time I did."

"Oh, I see, so maybe he backed out of his bid for you." Holly was quiet for a moment. "Wow, that's pretty romantic."

"But now it feels like he's gone again."

"Kestra, if he really cares about you, he'll be back. If not, then you should just forget him."

"I don't want to forget him."

"Forget who?"

They looked up to see Dan in the doorway.

"Oh, nobody," muttered Kestra. Dan had such a habit of popping in at the worst times.

"Well, I just came to tell you the electrician's here. You might want to walk around with him and show him where you need extra outlets, or additional lights and things."

"Okay." She tried to smile. It's not like it was Dan's fault. He grinned back at her, and she did her best to smile in response.

～ 14 ～

Kestra stepped into McKenzie's and felt like Jack should emerge from his office to greet her. Instead Greg stepped out. He smiled and extended his hand. Something was up. Greg was not usually this polite, at least not to her. Why had he asked her to stop in like this?

"Hello, Kestra. Long time, no see." He ushered her to a side table and sat down across from her. "You're looking really great. That Oregon sea air must agree with you."

She'd never seen him so friendly. Maybe, at last, she'd been cast out of the wicked stepmother role. It had always seemed so ridiculous. After all they were nearly the same age. She sighed.

"Thanks, Greg. I'm really happy to be back in Port Star. I guess I never was much of a city girl at heart—at least not after your dad died. Plus I must admit, the restaurant biz here was getting me down."

Greg folded his hands and cleared his throat. "Business isn't going real well, Kestra." He spoke slowly, as if the words were caught in his throat.

"Is that why you asked me here?"

He nodded. "I think I'll have to shut down the Portland restaurant."

"Oh, no—"

"It's just not pulling its weight."

"But it's only been a few months."

"I know, but I don't think the location's right, or maybe just bad timing—"

"Or maybe if you just went back to the way Jack used to—"

"Kestra, please don't start on me. We've been through this enough."

"I know, Greg, but if it's not working—"

"I didn't ask you up here for advice, Kestra."

"What then?"

"I need your help. I need you to cut me some slack."

"How?"

"I want to renegotiate our deal. I'm having a hard time making ends meet. I can't keep the business going and pay you off within the time we'd agreed."

"Greg, I already sold out for much less than my share was worth. If business is that bad, maybe you should get out, too. Maybe this isn't what you're cut out for, Greg. You don't need to try to fill your father's shoes. Have you ever stopped to consider what it is you really want?"

He looked her straight in the eye, and for the first time she saw Jack reflected in his face. The coloring was all different, but without a doubt she saw Jack.

"Please, Kestra. Can't you see? I feel like I've got to make this work. I have to show myself I can do it. I really think I can make it work, but it's hard right now. It will wipe me out to come up with the cash to pay off your share. Don't get me wrong, I'm grateful you decided to let me take full control, and I know you gave me a great deal. I just need more time to pull this together. Can you understand?"

She swallowed. "Yes, I think so. Tell me how you want to do this."

He pulled out some papers. She read through and quickly signed them. She knew she was losing more money, but this was Jack's only child, his own flesh and blood. What had she done to deserve half of the business anyway? And beyond that, it seemed as if Greg had changed. It seemed as if the business finally meant something to him. Maybe she could help him succeed. Maybe this was her way of thanking Jack.

He let out a deep breath and folded the papers. "Thanks, Kestra. I know we never got along before. I realize now it was mostly my fault, and I'm sorry for that. I resented you a lot. I blamed you for what was wrong between Dad and me." He looked down at the table, she knew it wasn't easy for him to admit that.

Kestra reached out and laid her hand on Greg's. "Your dad is probably smiling right now."

"I hope so." His eyes looked wet.

"So, what are you going to do now, Greg? What's your plan?"

"Well, I'll focus my attention on keeping the other restaurants going. I don't mind losing Portland, as long as I can make these work—only I have to do it my own way."

"I understand."

Greg smiled. "Enough about me. How's your business coming? Hey, maybe I've done you a favor by shutting down Portland. Who knows—maybe some business will trickle on over to the coast now."

She shook her head. "Well, it will be a while before I'm ready for any business. The house is still in the renovation stage now. But it's looking great. I hope you'll come out and see it when it's done, Greg."

"Sure, you bet I will. Then we can compare notes, and I can

tell you how to run your business." They both laughed.

"Say, Greg, I just thought of something. If you're shutting down Portland, what are your plans for all the new kitchen equipment you just put in?"

"Do you need it?"

"If you're getting rid of it, maybe we could make it part of this agreement. It might help balance things out."

"Sure, and I've also got a bunch of supplies from the changes I made in the other restaurants. Silverware, china, tablecloths—all the frills. It's all boxed up and just taking up space in the storage room. It's yours, if you'd like."

"I'd love it, Greg. It would mean a lot to take a piece of McKenzie's back to The Wise Man's House."

Greg stuck out his hand. "Then it's a deal, Kestra." They shook on it, and for some reason she didn't feel like she'd just been on the losing end of a business deal. She knew it meant less money, but that seemed small compared to what was just gained. She felt like Jack would have wanted it this way.

Kestra spent the next few days in Seattle. She and Holly had made an enormous shopping list before she'd left Port Star. It was full of things like light fixtures, plumbing accessories, flooring, and all kinds of hard-to-find renovation items. She'd never been to so many musty warehouses and factory outlets in her life, but in the end it was worth it. She found one warehouse on the waterfront that had just taken in some embossed copper sheeting, rescued from a condemned hotel. It would be perfect for the dining room ceiling. The little man behind the counter introduced himself as Mr. Vinnetti and guaranteed he'd have the sheeting refurbished and delivered to her within six weeks. He also promised to check into some copper light fixtures he'd seen at the same place. His interest in her project was encouraging, and he even told her about an outlet store down the road with a fantastic selection of cabinet hardware and plumbing accessories, all replicated from the turn of the century.

On her last day in Seattle she stopped by the cemetery to place some roses on Jack's grave. Right after his death, she had visited regularly. Later on she went only occasionally. Now it had been almost a year. The sky was clear and sunny, but the wind whipped in off the Sound and seemed to cut through her like a knife. She nestled the red roses up against the stone, hoping to shelter them from the wind. Jack had always liked red roses. She crouched down, wrapping her long woolen coat around her like a blanket. She'd purposely worn a pretty designer silk dress with matching pumps. It was the first time she'd dressed like that in ages, and it felt silly, but she'd done it for Jack. It was always important to him that she look just right. He never liked to see her in jeans, although since she'd moved to the coast, she seemed to live in jeans.

She wrapped her arms around her knees and shivered. She stared at the white marble stone, like her mother's, only bigger. A tear slid down her cheek, at first warm, then cold as ice, followed by another. For a change, it didn't bother her to cry. She knew these were good tears. The kind that washed away bitterness.

"Thanks, Jack," her voice cracked as she spoke out loud. "Thanks for three good years. Thanks for everything. I'll never forget you." The wind blew one of the roses free from the rest. She picked it up and stood, taking a moment to inhale its rich sweetness. Then she flung it high over her head and watched as the wind caught it and swooped it away.

15

Holly's car was parked in front of the house when Kestra pulled in. The rest of the work crew's pickups and cars were parked along the side. It felt good to be home, and it felt good to know she was home. It seemed like ages since she'd left. She couldn't wait to see what had been accomplished while she'd been away.

"Kestra," called Dan from his pickup. He unrolled some plans as he walked toward her. "I want you to see this design for rebuilding that fireplace mantle in the front room."

She studied the design. "It looks nice, Dan. But does the whole mantle really need to be completely replaced? I like the one that's already in there."

"But that wood is so smoke-blackened we'll never get it to look very good. I think this one would be much nicer. Can't you just picture it in a nice oak?"

"I don't know. I think the old one has character. Let me think about it, Dan. Right now, I just want to see my house."

"Hey, Kestra," yelled Holly from an upstairs window. "Give me about ten minutes before you come up, okay?"

"Don't worry, Holly," Dan called up. "I'll keep her busy with

113

the downstairs for a while."

"Sounds like you guys are taking over," called Kestra. "I'm gone less than a week and look what happens." She held up her hands helplessly.

"Come on and see what the plumber's been up to in the kitchen." Dan put his hand on her back and guided her around to the side door. She moved quickly and was glad to feel his hand slip away. At first the starkness of the kitchen startled her. But she remembered this was exactly as planned.

"Wow, looks like someone has been working in here." She walked over to where the butler's pantry had once been. "This makes it a lot larger, opened up like this. It's huge!"

"But it will get smaller when everything's back in. Come check out the layout of this kitchen once more. This will be your last chance to make any changes before the plumbing goes in."

"Let's see. Yes, I think it looks about right. I've had a slight change in plans though. I plan to use the kitchen from the Portland McKenzies. Greg's shutting it down this month. Oh, and you won't believe this copper sheeting I found to go on the ceiling of the kitchen. I had the best time scavenging all kinds of neat stuff."

"Oh, Kestra," he groaned. "That's just the kind of thing a contractor does not want to hear. It's a lot more work to put in that old stuff than it is to just buy new." He ran his fingers through his hair and rolled his eyes.

"But I don't want new, Dan. I told you from the start, I want the place to feel authentic. That copper is going to be beautiful, you'll see. And the kitchen equipment is new. The restaurant was only built last winter."

"Yeah, but the pieces might not fit just right in here. Do you know what sizes they are?"

"No, not exactly. But I've already arranged to have them

delivered next month. You can make them fit."

"You're crazy! You're having them shipped and you don't even know if they'll fit. How much are you paying for all this?"

She smiled. "Actually, they're free."

"Free? Come on, Kestra. Nothing is ever free."

"Well, not completely free. I sort of struck a deal with my stepson. Remember, I sold him my half of the restaurants. He was having a hard time, so we renegotiated our deal, and he threw in the restaurant equipment."

"I hate to think how much you lost on that little deal."

"Money isn't everything, Dan."

"It's certainly not everything to you. You know, Kestra, if you're going to make a serious go in business, you'd better start thinking more like a businesswoman."

"Thanks for the tip, Dan." She turned away. "I think it's been more than ten minutes. Now I want to see what Holly's been up to." She tried not to stomp off as she exited. Why did Dan have to be such a wet blanket when it came to her house? Sometimes it felt like he was taking over.

She tiptoed down the upstairs hallway to the bedroom on the end. When she cracked open the door, she couldn't believe the transformation. The floor and the woodwork had been refinished when she'd last seen this room, but that was all. Now all the painting was completed and the wallpaper nicely hung.

"It's beautiful, Holly. It looks so fresh and clean. This paper is lovely. It's so light and airy, and yet the pattern's so quaint and old-fashioned. I love it."

Holly beamed. "Matthew came over last night and helped me finish it. Come see the bathroom."

"It's perfect." Kestra ran her hand over the smooth paper. The delicate green vines trailed lightly over the creamy background.

"Look, there was even enough paper to do the linen closet."

Holly proudly opened the narrow closet. "Isn't it cute?"

Kestra hugged her friend. "Holly, this was so sweet of you."

"I was hoping you wouldn't mind. I didn't want to overstep any boundaries—"

"What—are you joking? I love it. I don't even know what to say—it's fantastic! And after talking to Dan, I needed some encouragement like this. Thanks so much!"

"Why? What did Danny Boy have to say?"

"Oh, same old thing. 'Why'd you buy that old stuff, it's easier to build with new, blah, blah, blah.' You know how he drones on and on." They both laughed.

"Well, Kestra, just remember—you're the boss. Dan is working for you. He's supposed to do what you want."

"Well, someone should remind him."

"That someone would be you, Kestra."

"I suppose. Hey, I've got some real treasures down in the car. I found these pale green glass knobs that'll be perfect on these cabinets. And I found a bunch of old Oriental carpets and some lace curtains at a flea market. I left them in Seattle to get cleaned and mended. I don't even know if they'll fit anywhere. You could always have them for your shop. I couldn't resist, they were practically giving them away."

"Lately you've been keeping me pretty well stocked, with the antiques you didn't think you'd want in here, and the funky fifties light fixtures you took out of the house."

"It's the least I can do to repay you for all your work. I mean look at this place." Kestra spun around admiring the room again. "It's absolutely beautiful, Holly. You even scrubbed the windows. I could practically move in."

"Actually, once the electrician finishes up, and you decide on your bathroom faucets, you probably could move in."

"Maybe, but I think I'll wait. I'm still enjoying my little cottage too much to leave just yet."

"Well, how about showing me all those treasures down in your car?"

Holly and Kestra spent almost two hours just getting the knobs installed onto the mahogany cabinets in the bathroom. Finally they stepped back to admire their handiwork and decided it was worth the effort. The afternoon shadows were lengthening, and the workers had already called it a day. Holly invited Kestra to join her and Matthew for dinner. But Kestra declined. She was so glad to be home, she didn't mind if all she ate was a bowl of soup.

Kestra stood in front of the bay window of the bedroom. The sun was slowly slipping into the sea, leaving a golden stripe right through the middle of the ocean. A few whispy clouds turned pink on the horizon. It wasn't flamboyant—just peaceful. She turned around for one last look at the room before daylight was gone. It was a very romantic room. It would be a nice room to share with someone—someone very special. She wondered about the past generations who'd dwelled in this house. Had they been happy? In love? Would she?

She gazed out the window until the last remnant of the light vanished before her eyes. She peered into the blackness, then out on the ocean she spotted what must have been the light of a trawler. She wondered how it would feel to be out on the ocean at night. Probably lonely. She knew what that felt like. But for some reason, she didn't feel lonely. Just alone, and it was all right to be alone. Because after all, God was with her. She wasn't really alone.

⌒ 16 ⌒

Riley had missed her. All evening he followed her around like a little copper shadow. Dan, true to his word, had taken care of the pup each day, but she could tell by Riley's golden brown eyes that he was glad she was back. Sometime during the night he climbed out of his basket and onto her bed. She decided to ignore it, just this one time. When she awoke, his warm little body was snuggled up next to her. She hoped she wasn't encouraging a bad habit, but he was so sweet and cute.

After breakfast and some quick housekeeping, she took Riley down to the beach for a romp. He loved to run and had no problem keeping up, although occasionally his oversized puppy feet got in the way, and he'd tumble head first into the sand. But it never phased him, he just hopped up and kept running. She enjoyed this time, too. She'd been on the cross-country team in high school but had almost forgotten how much she loved the freedom of running. She had increased her run a little each day, in order to help Riley get used to it. Her goal was to be able to make it clear to the Jetty and back by the end of summer. But she hadn't run for a whole week, and after a while her side started to throb so she decided to walk back.

It was a beautiful morning, one of those rare days in May when the ocean breeze seemed to have slept in, allowing the morning sun to send down its warmth without being whisked off to the sea. Kestra removed her running shoes and walked along the wet sand, not bothering to move as the tide washed up with its chilling waters against her feet. Riley ran back and forth barking at the little peaks of foam that fringed the tide. He chomped into a peak only to have the foam go up his nose and then disappear. He wheezed and shook his head back and forth in confusion.

"Riley, you silly dog!" She laughed and picked up a stick and threw it. This was still a new concept for Riley. She'd worked on it before, but he hadn't quite gotten it. However, this time he ran after the stick, picked it up, and brought it halfway back before he dropped it.

"Good!" She patted his head. "Now try it again. But bring it all the way back." She tossed the stick and this time he brought it back to her.

"Good boy!" she exclaimed. She threw it again and again, a little further with each throw. And each time he brought it back, tail wagging in delight.

After a while she grew tired of throwing the stick, but Riley still wanted to play. "Okay, one last big throw," she proclaimed. She held the stick and turned around and around hoping to get some momentum. Riley barked in excitement as she released the stick. He took off and she watched it soar in the air, but to her surprise it was going straight into the ocean.

"Stop, Riley!" she called, but it was too late. Riley had already plunged right in and was valiantly dog-paddling toward the stick. He was quickly flipped under by a wave. She ran toward him, heart pounding. Poor Riley! She saw his wet head pop out of the water with wide, fear-filled eyes, and then he was pulled under by another wave.

"Hold on, Riley!" she screamed as she ran through the surf toward him. She was quickly out to her waist and couldn't spot him for a long moment. Then she saw a wave toss him like a piece of driftwood. She reached in and grabbed him, pulling him toward her like a small child.

"Oh, Riley," she cried. "Are you okay?" He opened his eyes and looked at her. His little tongue came out and gently licked her cheek, and she burst into tears. "I'm so sorry. I didn't mean for you to go out in the water to get the stick." She cradled him in her arms and carried him back toward the beach. Next to the water's edge she noticed a bystander nearby. He had thrown down his jacket as if ready to lend a hand. The sun was behind him and she could only make out a silhouette, but something about him made her heart beat a little faster. And it was already racing.

"Are you okay?" he called. And she was certain she recognized the voice. As she came nearer, she knew it was Quin Larson.

"Quin, what on earth are you doing here?"

He smiled. "I was about to ask you the same thing."

Riley began to squirm in her arms, and she gently set him down. He shook off, splattering Quin with a healthy dose of sea water.

"Sorry about that." Kestra kneeled down before Riley and ruffled his wet coat. She looked up at Quin. "I just tried to drown my dog."

Quin's face looked puzzled.

"Well, not really. We were playing chase the stick, and my aim went haywire. But Riley showed his true loyalty by going after it, and then I had to go pull him out. I feel so horrible. I don't know what I'd have done if he'd drowned." She realized how she was babbling and paused. Quin picked his jacket up off the ground.

"Here, Kestra. You're shivering."

"I'll get it all wet." But he was already slipping it over her shoulders. It was still warm from his body, and she pulled it around her. "Thanks, Quin. So tell me, what are you doing here? Did you get my letter? I tried to explain in it how I hadn't gotten your first letter for two weeks."

"Yes, your letter was forwarded to me. Thank you for writing. I'd really been worried that I might've said something to give the wrong impression in my first letter. I'd written at a lonely moment. You know how that can go…"

She nodded, but wondered if she really knew. Was he trying to say he didn't mean the things he'd written in that first letter?

"My shoes are over there." She walked over and sat on the driftwood log and dried off her feet with her socks. Why was it whenever Quin was around she felt almost tongue-tied, almost like a school girl? Why couldn't she relax and be herself? Her shoelace had a knot in it and her fingers were still cold from her unexpected dip.

"Here," he reached for the shoe. "Let me help." He loosened the knot and handed it back. Their hands touched and their eyes met, and Kestra felt almost as if she couldn't breathe. He reached over and carefully moved a wet curl from her eyes.

"I didn't realize that was you in the water, and I couldn't exactly tell what was going on. I was about to jump in and lend a hand, but it looked like things were under control. I'm glad he's okay." He reached down and stroked Riley's head and smiled. She watched for the crinkles by his eyes. They were still there.

"Thanks. I felt so helpless for a split second. I couldn't see him in the water. I've never had a dog before, and it seems silly, but I really love this one." She reached down and fondled Riley's ear as he lay at her feet on the warm, dry sand, clearly exhausted.

"And he looks like a good dog, too. You say his name is Riley?"

"Yes, it's from my favorite author, Patrick O'Riley. I hope that's not disrespectful, but it's such a nice Irish name, you know, for an Irish Setter."

"Aye, lassie, it's a grand old name and a very good choice, even if it is for a dog." Quin's eyes twinkled as he spoke with an Irish brogue.

"Very good." She laughed. "And I speak from experience. My father was from Irish decent, and every once in a while he would put on a real Irish tongue. His parents came from Dublin, but they both passed on when I was little. I never really knew them, but they sounded nice, from what I heard anyway."

"I have some Irish roots myself."

"I thought with a name like Larson you'd be Scandinavian."

"Actually, my father was Swedish, but my mother is Irish."

"I see." Kestra looked out across the ocean. "So, Mr. Larson, what exactly brings you to this corner of the world?"

"Well, as it turns out, I'm still looking to rent a nice little cabin somewhere on the coast. Do you know of anything?"

"Really?" she turned and looked at him. "I thought you already had something lined up."

"I did, until I saw it. I was told it was a cabin with a view of the sea, but in reality it had a view of the back of a mobile home, a raggedy fence, and if you stood on a chair on a clear day, you might see about a square inch of ocean."

She laughed. "Well, I can do better than that. In fact, I have this little cottage that has been recently redecorated…"

"Really?" His tone didn't sound very excited. "Redecorated?" He spoke the word like he was imagining ruffles and lace.

She stood up. "Maybe you'd like to see it."

"Sure, do you think Riley is ready to travel?" He looked down at the sleeping dog, then bent over and scooped him up.

"You don't need to do—"

"It's okay, he's not very heavy. Now in a year or so, I might not want to carry him."

"Thanks, Quin." They walked along in silence. But it was a comfortable silence. Kestra caught a glimpse of Quin in the corner of her eye. He was holding the sleeping pup close to him and looking down. Kestra turned away and walked a little faster. What was she getting into?

Riley awoke just as they reached the top of the steps. Quin let him down and the pup scampered around his feet like they were best friends. Quin looked at the cottage and grinned.

"Well, at least you didn't change anything on the outside."

"You better come in before you write it off completely." She opened the door and stood back, thankful she'd cleaned this morning.

"This is nice." He nodded with approval. "Very, very nice, Kestra. But is someone living here?"

Her face reddened. "Well, uh, yes. I'm staying here right now, but the house is almost ready to live in—"

"Oh, I see. Well, actually I don't need a place until June. Did you plan to move into the house very soon? I don't want to force you out."

"No problem. It's almost ready and I can't wait to move in. Not that I don't like the cottage, but I'm excited to be in the house."

"I can understand that. Well, would you like me to sign any kind of agreement?"

"No, your word is good enough for me."

Quin extended his hand. "Fine, then let's shake on it." Her hand fit nicely into his and neither one of them let go for what seemed like a long moment. Finally she let her hand drop and turned away, her cheeks burning.

"How about a cup of coffee?" She went into the kitchen. "I

just ground some great smelling beans. I think it was called golden pecan or something, but it smells just like vanilla. And I have some shortbread cookies if you're interested." She wanted to keep babbling as she fumbled around for a coffee filter. Her heart was moving way too fast.

"That would be nice, Kestra." He walked over to the fireplace, his back to her. "You've really done a great job in here. When you told me you redecorated I guess I expected the worst. But I'm impressed."

"My friend, Holly, helped me out quite a bit. She has a real knack. I told her the kind of things I like, and she helped me to find them."

"Well, maybe if the restaurant business doesn't work out you and Holly could take up interior decorating."

She set two mugs of coffee on the table and went back for a plate of shortbread. "I'll keep that in mind. So where will you be in between now and June?"

"I have some business to take care of back east."

She wanted to ask what kind of business, but knew that was too nosy. And Quin certainly didn't seem one to disclose an overabundance of information. She, on the other hand, seemed to turn into an open book whenever he was around. Maybe she would have to watch herself. She didn't want to appear too interested.

"Do you have any plans for dinner tonight?" he asked as he pushed up the sleeve of his denim shirt and glanced at his watch.

"No." Was he asking her out for a date? Her heart beat a little faster.

"If I promised not to take you to Gil's Chowder House, could I entice you to join me?"

"Of course, I'd love to!"

"Shall I pick you up around six then?"

"That would be—" A loud knocking startled her.

"Hey, Kestra!" yelled Dan as he opened the front door. "Are you in here? Oh, I didn't know you had company, Kestra." Dan looked at Quin with open curiosity.

"Quin Larson," said Kestra. "This is Dan Hackett, my contractor."

"Contractor and friend," corrected Dan as he extended his hand to Quin.

"Nice to meet you," said Quin. "I look forward to seeing the work you've done on the house."

Dan frowned slightly. "Sure, come on over."

"I don't have time right now, but I'll be back." He turned to Kestra. "Six then?"

"Sure," she replied.

Quin nodded to them both and walked away.

"Who's he?" said Dan. "What is he to you?"

Kestra watched Quin walk away, then turned to Dan. "In answer to your first question, he used to live here. As for your second question—it's really none of your business!"

It just figured that Dan would pop in right now.

～ 17 ～

K estra, this is so exciting," gushed Holly. "Do you know where he's taking you? What are you going to wear?"

"I don't know. This is all so strange. I mean this is like my first real date since Jack…"

"Didn't you have dinner with Dan once?"

"That didn't count. It was just friends and business."

"I'm not so sure that Dan thought so."

"Well, Dan and I have discussed our relationship. I've tried to make it clear where I stand, Holly."

"I know, but the guy has a pretty thick head. You know how those Hacketts are." She laughed and turned to Kestra's tiny closet. "How do you manage to keep all your clothes in here?"

"I don't. A bunch of my stuff is stored. But believe me I'm looking forward to getting into the big house and that wonderful bedroom! In fact, I promised Quin that I'd be out of here by June. That's when he'll be needing it."

Holly lifted a brow. "Does Dan know about this?"

"What do you mean?" Kestra was getting tired of Dan's interference in her personal life.

"I mean as your contractor," Holly said the words as if she

were addressing a preschooler.

"Oh," Kestra nodded. "No, I haven't broke the news yet—"

"Hey, how about this?" Holly pulled out a bright coral silk dress.

"Too flashy." Kestra flopped onto the bed and closed her eyes. "I want something nice but understated."

Holly pulled out a denim jumper. "This?"

"Not that understated. I don't want to look like I just stepped off the farm."

"Are you always this difficult?"

Kestra laughed. "I don't know. I'm a little out of the habit of dating."

Holly stuck the jumper back in the closet and turned around. "Tell me. Just what do you really know about this guy, Kestra? He seems so mysterious. What does he do for a living? Why does he want to rent this cottage? Just who is he anyway?"

"He's Quin Larson. He's very nice. And for some reason I really, really like him."

"Oh, now, that really, really explains everything." Holly rolled her eyes and turned back to the closet. "Hey, how about this one?" She held up a dress that Kestra had bought in Seattle but had never worn. It was a heavy washed silk in a mossy shade of green.

"Hmm, let's see that." Kestra rose in interest. She held the dress in front of her and looked in the mirror.

Holly nodded. "Yep, I think that's the one. Understated, yet elegant. And it really looks nice with your eyes. Maybe you should put your hair up that way you do sometimes—is it a french twist?"

"Good idea, and maybe some pearls…"

"Well, I can see my job here is done, my dear. And as it is, I happen to have plans myself tonight." She smiled slyly.

"A date with Matthew?"

"Not exactly. He invited me to his Bible study group."

"That sounds pretty serious. Is that kind of like taking you home to meet Mom and Dad?"

Holly laughed. "I wish! But the truth is, I'm really just enjoying his friendship right now. And if it turns into something more, that'll be just fine!"

"It sounds like a good way to start a relationship, Holly. Now off with you! Bible study or not, you'll want to look your best, too!"

"Right you are!" called Holly as she opened the door and waved. "And I hope you have a good time with Quin tonight."

Kestra decided to take her time getting ready. It was one of those occasions that was worth stretching out—worth anticipating. She smiled as she squirted on a little of her favorite perfume. This was fun! She slipped on some moss-colored suede pumps that went with the dress and looked in the mirror. It was perfect! Riley sat and looked at her with loyal brown eyes.

"What do you think, boy?" He wagged his tail and wiggled with delight. "I'll bet you're thinking more about your own dinner plans, aren't you, pal?"

Just as she set down his bowl of food, she heard a knock on the door and suddenly she got a case of butterflies that she never would have thought possible a few months ago. She felt very vulnerable, and it was unsettling. *Lord, help me to calm down,* she prayed silently as she quickly washed her hands and answered the door.

Quin handed her a small bouquet of irises with a shy smile. "I saw these in town and thought you might like them."

"I love irises. Thank you. Just let me put them in water and then we can go." She glanced at him as she filled a crystal vase and quickly arranged the dark purple blooms. He was wearing chinos with a nice dark jacket. Understated, but elegant. He paced back and forth in the tiny living room. Could it be that he was nervous, too? He just didn't seem the type to be uncomfortable in any situation. But then what did she really know about him?

They drove up the coastal highway toward the small town of Seal Cove. It was prettier than Port Star, and developers had capitalized on its natural charm, building high-priced condos and a very nice resort. Kestra told Quin all about the progress on the house. She explained to him how she had gotten the copper ceiling for the kitchen, and he thought it sounded perfect. She told him about the antiques that Jack had stored away and how it was like Christmas when they arrived.

The sun was just going down as they were seated by the window at a candlelit table.

"It sounds like things are really working out for you, Kestra," said Quin as he picked up his water goblet in a mock toast. "The Wise Man's House is really coming along. I'm very happy for you."

"I've always wanted to tell you thanks."

"What do you mean?"

"Well, I suspect you had something to do with me getting the house. And it really means a lot to me. Thank you."

"Oh, I'm just a small player in the scheme of things. Someone else is directing this for you."

"I know what you mean. I really believe God is bringing all this together. It's just so amazing how all the pieces keep falling into place. But I just can't figure out why God cares that much to do this for me. I mean, look at me, I'm nobody. I haven't even lived a very good life—not that I've done anything horribly wrong, but I haven't really done anything especially noble or good. Not that I couldn't. Oh, here I go babbling again. I'm sorry…"

"Don't be sorry. You're not babbling. I enjoy hearing you talk. I find your honesty very refreshing."

She looked down at her plate. She wished he'd talk about himself for a change, but she didn't know quite how to get him started. Didn't most men enjoy talking about themselves? Quin was a hard one to figure.

"I noticed some drawings when I first met you. Are you an artist?"

He laughed. "No, it's just a hobby. It helps me to relax and unwind. But my sketches aren't anything I'd want anyone to see."

"I've often thought I'd like to take some sort of art class myself, but I just never got around to it. Actually, lately I've been thinking I should take a cooking class."

"For the restaurant?"

This time she laughed. "No, I don't think even the best class could bring me to that level. No, I'll have to hire a chef for the restaurant. I want to get someone really good. I think that'll be part of the draw. I'd like to advertise The Wise Man's House in the Portland papers to start off, and I think if I get a chef with a big enough name, it might encourage people to drive over. It is a pretty drive. Do you think that makes sense?"

"Sure it does. You seem to have a pretty good business head, Kestra. I think you'll do well."

"Thanks. Not everyone thinks so."

"Well, you shouldn't worry so much about what other people think." His face grew serious as he looked out the window. She followed his gaze in time to see a strip of rosy light lingering on the horizon, then quickly become swallowed up by the sea.

She took a bite of scampi and wondered if he thought she was too concerned about other people's opinions. Was she? Or was she just overreacting to a casual comment? Jack used to say she was overly sensitive about things.

Soft piano music began to play and Kestra looked over to see a small dance floor off to one side of the restaurant. She hadn't noticed it earlier. She and Jack used to dance. He had been a good dancer.

They lingered over dessert and coffee, listening to the old tunes from the forties and fifties. A few couples had begun to dance slowly to the music, and Kestra longed for Quin to ask her, but he seemed to have no interest. Finally, he made the motions to leave and she picked up her purse.

"Would you like to dance?" he asked half apologetically. "I'm not much of a dancer, but I can give it a whirl if you like."

She smiled up at him. "That would be nice."

And it was. It was heavenly. Feelings she had almost forgotten stirred in her as she felt his hand grow warm on the small of her back. And once again, she thought about how well her small hand fit inside his larger one. She wanted the song to go on forever. But too soon it came to an end. And then it was time to go.

They drove in silence. The moon played light and shadow games with the clouds over the ocean. She leaned back and enjoyed the soothing sounds of classical music from the CD he had slipped in. Well, at least she wasn't babbling. It had been an almost perfect night. What more could she want?

He walked her to the door and took her hand in his again. "Thank you for going out with me tonight. I really had a great time."

"Me, too," she murmured as she looked into his face. The golden glow of light from inside the cottage illuminated his eyes with warmth. She had never been kissed by a man with a beard. She wondered what it would feel like. Would it be scratchy? Would it tickle? She didn't care.

"Good night, Kestra. I'll see you in June." He released her hand and turned away. She went into the house, closed the door, and leaned against it. She took in a deep breath and willed her heart to stop its mad pounding. Her sensible side sighed in relief that he hadn't kissed her. But the rest of her cried out in disappointment.

~ 18 ~

hat's this I hear about you renting the cottage out to some stranger and needing to move into the house by June?" demanded Dan.

Kestra set her spade aside and frowned up at him without standing. "Where did you hear that?" She spoke slowly, studying his face as she fingered the loose dirt. Of course, news traveled fast in town. But how did Dan always seem to have some special radar honed onto her business?

"Matthew Porter told me."

She turned back to the ivy and geraniums she had just potted and patted the soil into place. She loved the pungent smell of geraniums. She poured some water from the watering can and sighed. The sun on her back was warm and there was hardly a breeze. It could have been a perfect morning—

"Kestra, are you going to answer me?"

"What?" She stood and brushed potting soil from her jeans and looked at him. "Yes, it's true. I figured I could move into the finished wing—"

"You figured! You figured! Look, Kestra, it's just not that simple! The electrical work isn't even finished, and the inspector has to be scheduled to come, and the kitchen can't possibly be ready by then—"

"I can get by without a kitchen."

"Just who is this guy anyway? And what's the big hurry? You're not hurting for money are you? Why do you need to rent out the cottage so soon anyway?" His face was dark and stormy.

Riley romped up and nipped at Dan's bootlace, giving it a playful tug. Dan gave a quick kick, catching the pup right in the nose. Riley let out a yelp and looked up with startled hurt eyes.

"Dan Hackett!" Kestra bent over to check Riley. "Don't you dare kick my dog, you big bully!"

"Don't forget that's the dog *I* gave you. Come here, Riley ol' boy. I'm sorry, I didn't mean to bop you in the snout." He scratched the dog behind the ears and stood with a sheepish expression. Kestra shook her head.

"I intend to rent out the cottage in June, and it's none of your business why! If you can't have the house ready for me to move into the main section then, I'll just have to see if I can bunk with Holly for a while. I've already made an agreement."

"What do you mean, an agreement? Did you sign anything?"

She rolled her eyes. "No, but we shook on it."

Dan laughed cynically. "Well, then just tell him you can't do it. Tell him you were wrong, that the cottage is not available after all."

She glared at him. "Don't tell me how to live my life, Dan Hackett. You may be my contractor, but that's all! So why don't you just butt out! Furthermore, I expect you to get that wing ready by June!" She turned and stomped away. There he was, talking about contracts, when all she and Dan had was a "gentleman's agreement." Maybe she should just fire him and be done with this nonsense! She went into the cottage and slammed the door.

After an hour of fuming and furious cleaning, the small cottage shone. There wasn't a speck of dust left anywhere. She looked around, threw down her dust cloth, and slumped into a chair. She drummed her fingers on the worn pine table and stared at the vase of graceful irises. Last night seemed like a dream now. If only life could be like that always. She stared out the window at the warm spring day. She wanted to be out there, yet she felt like a captive in her own home. As much as she wanted to go out and finish planting flowerpots, she didn't want to take the chance of another confrontation with Dan.

Why did she even let him get to her like this? It was moments like these that made her long for her mother. How comforting it would be to sit here and pour out her heart to someone who really cared. Of course, there was Holly, but she was working today. Besides, she couldn't make too many demands on their friendship right now. Holly had Matthew in her life.

Kestra glanced at her Bible still sitting on the table. She'd taken to reading in the Gospels lately, and it had quickly become an encouraging part of her daily routine. She tried to recall exactly what she'd read just this morning. When it finally came to her, she had to laugh out loud. Of course, it would be about forgiveness! It was the part where Jesus told his disciples to forgive seven times seventy. She wondered how many times that would actually add up to. Surely, Dan Hackett had already used up more than twice that amount! But in her heart, she knew what the point was—she needed to keep on forgiving him.

"God, please help me," she prayed without hope. "It feels like Dan Hackett is my cross to bear in life. Please, please, help me to forgive him. I really need your help because I don't want to forgive him." She sat for a long moment, then finally took in a deep breath and let it out slowly. In the same moment, it felt like a huge weight was lifted from her.

"Thank you," she whispered. She looked at the clock. It was eleven-thirty. Since it was Saturday, Dan probably didn't have a crew working with him. She peeked outside to see if any other vehicles were parked by the house, but only saw Dan's big four-wheel drive. She heard hammering from inside the house. Poor Dan, here he was working on his Saturday and all she could do was chew him out and demand he get the main section done by June. It was surprising he hadn't just walked off.

She went back in the cottage and quickly made some sandwiches. She packed these into a basket with fruit, drinks, and some brownies she had made yesterday. Food made a good peace offering. She walked over to the house. It was looking good on the outside. So different from just a few months back. It wouldn't be long until the landscapers could get started. She carried the basket around the back side of the house, to the sun-drenched patio on the south end. She'd already hauled some cheap plastic patio furniture over here for the workers to use for breaks. She looked forward to the day she could replace it with something more substantial and better looking, but for now it was handy. She set the basket on the plastic table, then slipped into the house.

It was cool and dark inside, and she could hear the echo of hammering coming from upstairs. She tiptoed through the kitchen and dining room, admiring all the progress that had been made lately. Each day her anticipation for living here heightened. Even if Quin hadn't asked to rent the cottage, she would still be pushing to get settled in here. Finally, she spotted Dan bent over at the top of the landing.

"Hi, there," she called meekly from the bottom of the stairs. He stood and peered over the railing down at her.

"What do you want now?"

She walked up the stairs. "What are you working on?"

"Well, I figure if Ms. McKenzie plans to live up here, I better make sure she won't fall through the floor right here. I'm putting in some new subfloor so the floor guy can come on Monday and replace the parquet floor up here. You should have seen how rotten the original boards had worn."

"Looks good now."

"No, it doesn't. It just looks like subfloor."

"Yes, but you're doing a good job with it. Anyway, I didn't come up here to argue. In fact..." she paused. This was hard. "I wanted to apologize to you."

His eyes opened wide. "Really?"

She nodded and continued as if she had rehearsed the words. "Yes, I'm sorry I lost my temper at you. And to make amends, I brought you some lunch." She forced a stiff smile.

"All right! Well, I guess I should make you mad more often." He grinned mischievously.

She scowled. "Don't press your luck, bud!"

As they ate, she felt him study her. It made her uncomfortable and she wondered if this act of reconciliation had given him the wrong impression.

"What made you decide to apologize for losing your temper, Kestra? I mean, I've seen you lose your temper dozens of times, but I don't remember you ever saying you were sorry."

She took a sip of soda. "Well, I can't really take the credit. It was something I read in the Bible, and I guess God prompted me a little." She had never talked to Dan this openly before about God. She wondered what he might think now.

He scratched his head and looked puzzled. "Somehow I just never took you for a very religious woman, Kestra. I know you believe in God and have high standards and stuff. But you mean to say that you really *read* the Bible?"

"Actually, I haven't been much of a Bible reader until lately. But I really do find a lot of comfort in it. There's some pretty good stuff in there. You'd be amazed at how it relates to everyday life. In fact, I wouldn't be talking to you right now if I hadn't read it this morning."

"Who would have thought?" Dan shook his head slowly. "So do you go to church and everything? Are you planning on doing anything outrageous like becoming a nun?"

"No, I'm not even Catholic, silly! I have been thinking about looking for a church, but I'm not sure where to start. I know Matthew has a church he likes in Harrison, but I thought I'd check out the local ones first."

"I've been thinking about going to church."

"Really? You? Why do I find that hard to believe?"

"No, seriously. I've been considering going back to St. John's. I took Amber there a couple of times. Melinda never wanted to go. In fact, I even asked Amber to come with me for last Easter, but she said she didn't want to. I think Melinda has her completely brainwashed now anyway." He looked down.

"That's too bad, Dan. I'm sorry. I'm sure it's not easy. Maybe in time Amber will see things differently."

"Hey," he brightened up. "Why don't you come with me to St. John's?"

She hesitated.

"Come on, Kestra. You said you wanted to check out the local churches. St. John's is one of the biggest and oldest."

And snootiest, she thought. "I know. Remember, I went with you and your folks at Christmas and Easter a couple of times."

"Sure. So why don't you come again. How about it? I'll pick you up at ten-thirty. I'm pretty sure the service still starts at eleven. Okay?"

He looked so hopeful, and she could think of no gracious way to back out. "Okay," she said reluctantly. She had a feeling she was going to regret this. She packed up the lunch things and stood. How had she gotten into this? Was this what God wanted?

"Thanks, Kestra." His face was beaming. "Now, I'm off to fix the castle for my little princess."

She stared at him in horror. "Dan—"

"Just kidding, Kestra."

He turned and walked away, but his words still made her uneasy. She told herself it was just his weird humor, but it still left her with an uncomfortable feeling. She hoped she hadn't encouraged him in the wrong way.

The next day, Dan was there at ten-thirty, right on the dot. He seemed uncomfortable in a gray suit that looked like it had been hanging in the closet for the past few years.

She had carefully selected her cream-colored linen suit with a designer scarf tucked tastefully around her neck. Her buck-skin pumps matched her hose and purse perfectly. It was an outfit Jack would have approved of. It looked classy and smelled of money. She knew it was silly and vain, but she wanted to impress the St. John's crowd. She even hoped the elder Hacketts might be there. Mrs. Hackett had always looked down on her. Dan's church was composed primarily of business people and those wanting to climb Port Star's little social ladder. She wondered why she even cared at this point in life. After all, she was a wealthy businesswoman. Certainly she could hold her head up around them now.

Dan parked across the street from the big brick church. She looked forward to seeing the jewel-toned stained glass windows from inside the sanctuary again. But when they walked through the big oak doors she suddenly felt very nervous. Several people nodded and waved to Dan, eyeing her with open curiosity. By now, everyone in town knew who she was, and probably they were speculating about her relationship with Dan. She knew that most of them remembered her from childhood days. And it felt like many of the town's elite still treated her like cheap trash. But then, this was church.

"Good morning, Dan," said Stanley Josephson. Stanley owned the hardware store and was good friends with Dan's dad. His wife, Helen, stepped up and looked at Kestra with arched brows.

"My, my, it's little Kestra O'Brian. I'd heard you were back in town. How nice that you've already managed to hook up with Dan here." Her tone was cold and arrogant, and her disapproval was obvious. She turned to Dan. "I would think you could at least bring little Amber to church with you sometime—"

"Dan!" called a shrill female voice from the foyer. Kestra looked over at Mrs. Hackett rushing their way. She was as rotund as ever and almost seemed to ooze out of her floral polyester dress. As usual she wore spiky, strappy shoes that seemed unable to support the bulk of her weight. "Oh, how nice to see you at church, Son. I was just saying to your father how nice it would be if you would come back to St. John's. What a fine way to get your life back on track." She didn't even look at Kestra. "Your father's just parking the car and he should be—"

"Mom," interrupted Dan. "I'm sure you remember Kestra." Mrs. Hackett's forehead wrinkled as she turned to see.

"Of course, I didn't realize that was you, dear." She looked at Kestra, carefully scanning every detail. "Well, it appears you've grown up into a nice young lady." Kestra smiled stiffly. She felt like an insect under a magnifying glass.

"Thank you, Mrs. Hackett. You're looking well as always."

Mrs. Hackett began waving frantically. "Over here, Howard. Come see! Our Dan is here!"

Mr. Hackett walked over slowly. He had aged a lot in the past ten years. His hair was completely white and his face looked different. Almost softer. "Hello, Dan," he said extending a hand. "Good to see you, Son." He looked at Kestra as if he couldn't exactly recall how he knew her. Then he broke into a sunny smile, and Kestra actually felt the first ray of warmth since she'd walked into the building. "Why, if it isn't Kestra O'Brian!" He reached out and squeezed her hand. "Welcome back to Port Star, dear. It's so good to see you! Come, come and sit with us." Mrs. Hackett seemed to bristle but she smiled politely. And they all walked to the same pew the Hackett family had occupied for the last several decades.

Mr. and Mrs. Hackett sat next to the aisle with Dan next to his mother. The organ music played formally, and people began to quickly find their seats, almost as if they had all been previously assigned in some grand seating chart on high.

"Is your dad's health okay?" whispered Kestra. "He looks different than I remember."

"He had a stroke a couple years back. It really slowed him down at first, but he's doing all right now."

Kestra paid close attention to all parts of the service, hungry for any morsel of spiritual encouragement. But it seemed all the standing, sitting, and reading from the prayer books was lifeless. The only thing she really enjoyed was the singing. The old hymns felt more genuine than the rest of the liturgy, and she was disappointed when they only sang a few songs. She reminisced over her church in Seattle where much of the service had been focused on singing praise songs. She'd taken it for granted then. How she missed it now!

Even when the pastor preached it felt old and dusty and meaningless. And he didn't read a single Scripture from the Bible. She hated to be so judgmental, but she knew without a doubt this was not what she was looking for in a church. Even if the people had treated her better, she still wouldn't have felt at home. And it was a relief.

As he drove from the church, Dan asked her to join him at his folks' for lunch. She declined, saying she had a headache. It was the first time she'd been thankful for a headache.

She started to climb out of the pickup as soon as Dan pulled up by the cottage, but he put his hand on her arm. "Wait, Kestra. I need to talk to you."

She looked at him in alarm. "What?" She braced herself, and silently prayed: *Please don't let it be about our relationship. Please don't let him pull out a ring.*

He leaned over and opened the glove box. She swallowed and watched. He removed a stack of papers and laid them in her lap.

"I know we had a handshake agreement, Kestra. But I'm concerned. That isn't a very fair way to do business with you. You need something in writing that guarantees I will perform the work you have asked me to do. So I got this written up."

She sighed in relief. "Do you want me to go through this now?"

"Sure, it shouldn't take long."

She flipped through the papers and scanned them. It seemed to make sense and she was eager to be done with it. He handed her a pen and she signed.

"Thanks, I'll make a copy for your records."

"Sure." She opened the door and jumped out of the truck, waving as she ran up to the porch. She knew he wanted an invitation to come in, but she felt like she'd already gone beyond the call of her Christian duty just by spending the morning with him.

She was more than happy to rid herself of her church clothes, and she laughed at her foolishness when she considered how carefully she'd dressed just a few hours earlier. She gladly pulled on her worn jeans with holes in the knees and a faded sweatshirt, then took Riley down for a romp on the beach. The sky and the ocean were clear and blue, and just a breath of a breeze ruffled her hair. She breathed in the fresh air and decided she could just as easily worship God down here in all this glory as in a church. And that's what she did.

~ 19 ~

Kestra spotted Holly's car pull up just as she climbed the last steps up from the beach. She waved and walked over to see what brought her friend out today.

"Hey you, I've been trying to call for two days," said Holly as she stepped out of the car. "Have you ever considered joining the age of modern technology and getting an answering machine?"

"I have one somewhere, I just haven't unpacked it yet. What's up?"

"I wanted to find out how the date went. I've been just dying of curiosity since Friday!"

"I was home all night, last night. Didn't hear my phone ring once. How come you didn't call then?" Kestra teased. "Let me guess—big date with Matthew?"

"Well, as a matter of fact, yes. But first, let's talk about you! Hey, have you got anything to eat in there? I haven't even had lunch yet and I'm starved."

"Actually, I haven't eaten either. Let me put some fresh water out for Riley and then I'll see what I can scrounge up."

Kestra found the makings for a chef salad, and a partial loaf of french bread which she sliced and melted cheese on. Holly helped and soon they set a decent lunch on the table.

"So you guys actually danced?" asked Holly between bites.

"Well, only one dance. But it was very nice."

Holly nodded. "Sounds pretty romantic. But still you haven't really told me anything about this guy. Like what he does for a living. Has he ever been married? Ever murdered anyone? You know, little insignificant things like that."

Kestra shook her head. "You sound so suspicious. Why can't he just be a nice guy who doesn't like to talk about himself?"

"All guys like to talk about themselves!"

"Even Matthew?"

"Well, now Matthew's different…"

"Aha! So it is possible for a guy to be a decent person and not want to talk about himself."

"Yes and no, but at least I know what Matthew does for a living. I know where he lives. I know he has a family. And actually, I even found out why such a great guy is still single. So you see, I'm way ahead of you there."

"Yes?" Kestra leaned over. "So why is he single?"

Holly shook her head slowly. "Actually it's a pretty sad story. Do you really want to hear?"

"I guess so. I mean, I can tell you're getting serious about him. He's not dying or anything is he?" Kestra pushed her empty plate aside and looked at her friend intently.

"No, that's not it, thank goodness. Actually, he was married for eight years. He married his high-school sweetheart about twelve years ago. Her name was Sarah, and they had a little boy named Benjamin. Benjamin was only three—" Holly's voice choked a little but she went on. "Sarah and Benjamin were killed in a head-on collision by a drunk driver."

"Oh, that's so tragic. Poor Matthew."

"Yes, it just about killed him. He wasn't a Christian at the time, and he was so bitter. He started drinking. And one night he was driving under the influence and narrowly missed hitting another car. He totaled his pickup and spent two months in the hospital. He couldn't believe how he was guilty of the same thing that killed his family. That's when he called out to God."

"Wow, what an amazing story. You'd never guess he'd experienced such a tragedy."

"I know what you mean. He's such an upbeat person. He just loves kids, and he even leads a youth group in his church. In fact, I went to his church today, and it was great! I want to go again tonight. They have an evening worship service. I thought I'd see if you wanted to come along, too."

"That sounds great, Holly. Actually, I've been longing to get plugged into a good church. You'll never believe what I did this morning." She went on to explain, in colorful detail, the fiasco of going to Dan's church. Before long they were both laughing so hard that tears were running down their cheeks.

Kestra went with Holly to Matthew's church that night. It felt like going home. Before the evening service was over she decided it was well worth the forty minute drive to get there. Matthew introduced Holly and Kestra to several other people who were from Port Star.

"I was just telling Karen Green, here, that you folks should organize a midweek Bible study group like the one we have over here," said Matthew.

Karen was a middle-aged woman with dishwater blond hair. She looked down at her hands and then spoke in a quiet voice. "I would love something like that, but who could we get to lead it?"

Holly chimed in. "I'd like to come, but I sure wouldn't want to lead it."

"Well, maybe you could host the group at your place, Holly," suggested Matthew with a twinkle in his eye. "And if anyone is interested, I would be glad to lead it. At least I could get you folks started."

"That would be great," said Kestra. She'd be happy to be involved in a group led by Matthew. He seemed to have such depth.

"Well, when do we start?" asked Karen.

"How about Wednesday?" suggested Holly. "You don't have a midweek service here do you?"

"No, we encourage people to meet in fellowship groups during the week," said Matthew. "Wednesday works for me. And feel free to invite anyone you'd like." He turned to Kestra with a smile. "You might want to invite Dan Hackett." She smiled back through gritted teeth and nodded. It was the last thing she wanted to do, but she could at least think about it.

"Thanks for taking me tonight, Holly," said Kestra as she got out of the car. "I'm already looking forward to the Bible study—"

"Are you really going to invite Dan?" Holly's brows lifted in a teasing manner.

Kestra shook her head. "Tell you what. I'll pray about it. Okay?"

"Okay by me. See ya!"

Workers were on the job first thing in the morning. Kestra decided to stay out of their hair. She knew Dan was trying to meet her June deadline, and she didn't want to get in the way. Besides, she had lots to do now. On Monday, she worked on refinishing furniture. Then she met with the landscapers to plan the layout of the grounds. On Wednesday morning she realized that she hadn't invited Dan to the Bible study yet. She really didn't want to, but she also didn't want to have to tell Matthew that she hadn't. Finally, by late afternoon, she succumbed to the guilt and walked over to the house.

She found Dan upstairs putting some new trim on a section of hallway wall that had just been replastered.

"This is looking really good, Dan," she said with approval. "It looks to me like I could be in here even before June."

"So you're not going to back out of that deal?"

"I told you I wasn't."

He sighed in exasperation. "You are so darn stubborn, Kestra."

"Stubborn? This is my house! This is my—" she stopped herself. She wasn't going to lose control of her temper. It had cost her too much last time. "Actually, I didn't come over to talk about the house. I came over to invite you to something."

His eyes lighted up. "Sure, what is it?"

"Holly is going to have a Bible study at her place. Matthew Porter will lead it, and we'll meet every Wednesday. Actually it was Matthew who thought you might be interested."

"A Bible study?" Dan scratched his head with a frown. "You mean you sit around and read the Bible together?"

She nodded. "I think people talk and share and stuff, too. And knowing Holly there will probably be something good to eat."

"Talk and share about what?"

"Oh, I don't know. About how they feel about what they read. I don't know…"

"It sounds like one of those touchy feely groups to me. I don't think so, Kestra. Are you sure you want to go? It sounds a little weird to me. It's not really your thing, is it?"

She stifled her irritation. "Well, I'm looking forward to it," she said a little too curtly. "And I'm sorry you're not interested, Dan." She turned and walked down the stairs.

"Well, you don't have to get mad about it."

"I'm not mad," she called back, trying to sound pleasant.

Holly's place, as she expected, was cheerful and inviting with good smells coming from the kitchen. A vase of fresh flowers adorned the small dining table, and soft music floated from the stereo.

148

"I came early in case there's anything I can do to help," called Kestra as she laid her jacket in Holly's bedroom.

"I think I'm okay. Here, why don't you set this plate of cookies out on the table. I'm not sure if we have refreshments before, after, or during. But I'm sure Matthew will know. I don't know why, but I feel sort of nervous. This is all new to me."

"Me, too, but I think it'll be fine."

Soon there were nine people crammed into Holly's tiny living room. Matthew led the group through the first half of the first chapter in Ephesians. He shared about what those words meant to him, how he finally realized how much God loved him, and how God helped him to escape from the bitterness that was eating him alive. He talked about how it felt to be stuck in a hospital bed right after the death of his wife and son. And finally he shared about how he now asked God to help him daily in his life.

Kestra shared, too. She told about how her life had hit a dead end and how she had become so depressed. Then she told about how God had miraculously given her the Wise Man's House. She didn't share the part that Quin played in this. But then she still wasn't sure about where he fit in, and besides that didn't change anything about how God was leading her now.

One by one everyone else shared. Everyone except for Karen Green—the one who had first spoken up about her need for this kind of group.

"Karen," began Matthew in a kind voice. "You're awfully quiet tonight. Is there anything you'd like to share. Any questions?"

Suddenly, Karen burst into tears. Between sobs she choked out the story of how her husband had abandoned her and their teen-aged daughter just a few months back. He'd left Karen for another woman. She told about how her daughter's grades had plummeted, and she'd gotten involved with all the wrong friends, and so Karen had decided to move them to a new town.

"Now Page says she hates me—that I've ruined her life by moving here." Holly handed her a Kleenex. "Page is threatening to run away, and I don't know what to do. She's only sixteen—" She dropped her head and continued to sob.

"Let's pray," said Matthew softly. It was awkward at first, but one by one they all prayed for Karen and Page. Finally, Matthew said "amen" and the room was quiet.

Karen lifted her head and Kestra thought she saw a trace of hope. "Thank you," she whispered.

People started drifting toward the kitchen for cookies and drinks. Kestra moved over to the couch next to Karen. An idea had just hit her, it was almost like an inspiration, but she wasn't sure if it was really the right thing or not. She prayed a silent prayer and then began to speak.

"Karen, does Page have any plans for the summer?"

"You mean besides running away?" Karen sniffed and tried to smile.

"What I'm wondering is—do you think she'd like to work for me this summer? You see, I'm trying to remodel this house and start this restaurant, and there's so much work to setting it up and everything, I could really use some help."

"You mean it?" Karen's red-rimmed eyes opened wide. "Oh, that would be—" She cut herself short and her gaze fell back to her lap. "But you haven't even met her yet. She—she's changed so much recently—she's not exactly your ordinary girl—you might not want—"

"Why don't I do an interview with her? How about Saturday? Let's just see how it works out. She may not even want the job. But it's worth a try isn't it?"

"Oh, yes, of course! It would be such an answer to my prayers." Karen grasped Kestra's hand. "Even if it doesn't work out, thank you for asking."

On Friday, Kestra found a postcard in her mailbox from Quin. Her heart beat a little faster as she quickly scanned his words. She hoped he hadn't changed his mind about coming. She sighed as she finished it. No, he was just thanking her for their dinner date and saying he looked forward to seeing her in June. She hadn't even looked at the front of the postcard long enough to see where it was from. She flipped it over. It was from Ireland! She looked back at the stamp and sure enough the postmark was from Dublin. Now what in the world was he doing there? He had mentioned nothing about it last week. He hadn't even said anything in his short note about what he was doing on the other side of the world. How strange!

Kestra had arranged to meet Page at Claire's Coffee Shop at ten. Karen and Page lived in a little apartment downtown and the coffee shop seemed convenient. Kestra arrived a few minutes before ten and sat down in a corner booth. She ordered a cup of coffee and waited, watching the door. A couple of girls came in, and Kestra looked closely to see if one of them might be Page. She had expected Page to come alone, but she wasn't sure, and had no idea what Page looked like. These girls both had blond hair, one had a long pony-tail and the other girl wore hers loose over her shoulders. Both girls wore shorts and had a pretty good start on a tan for the middle of May. They sat down at the counter, laughing and chatting. Neither of them even looked her way. At ten-fifteen the door opened again and another girl walked in. Her hair was an unnatural color of black and cut badly. The waiflike girl wore oversized dirty jeans and a torn plaid shirt. The girls at the counter whispered and stared, and the girl openly scowled back. Surely this wasn't Page!

The girl pushed up a limp shirt sleeve and checked what looked like a man's wristwatch, the oversized silver band dangling from her skinny wrist. She looked around the room with a frown, then spotted Kestra in the corner booth and cautiously shuffled over. Kestra was shocked. How could she trust someone who looked like this to work for her? She prayed a silent prayer, then waved in acknowledgment.

"Are you Page?" she asked with what she feared was a forced smile.

The girl nodded with serious eyes and a straight mouth. It seemed she was trying to ignore the high-pitched snickers that trickled from the lunch counter. Kestra didn't allow her eyes to move in that direction, and instead smiled again. This time it wasn't forced. Unexpectedly, Kestra's heart twisted in sympathy toward this strange girl.

"Come and sit down. Would you like a soda or anything?" Kestra caught the eye of the waitress walking by.

"Coffee," said Page to the waitress. "Black."

"Well, you must know that I'm Kestra. I'm sure your mom told you that I need help this summer…" She continued to explain what sort of work it was, talking too much and saying very little. The girl nodded as she poured several tablespoons of sugar into her coffee.

Kestra tried not to stare at the little gold post that pierced Page's right nostril or to count how many gold rings were in her ears. Instead she looked straight into Page's sad eyes. And there she saw a picture of herself as a young girl. Perhaps her pride had driven her to hide her pain better, but it had been there just the same.

Kestra took a sip of her now lukewarm coffee and wondered what more she could say. Page showed little interest in working for her. She asked no questions. Offered no information. Maybe this was all a big mistake. Maybe it would be best for both of them just to walk away. Page could represent more trouble than Kestra was willing to take on.

"You don't want me, do you?" said Page, leaning forward and looking her evenly in the eye. "I scare you, don't I?"

Kestra didn't know what to say. She took a deep breath. "Yes, Page, you scare me."

A sad gleam of satisfaction crossed Page's dark eyes. She looked down at the spoon she was jiggling in her hand. Her fingers were long and thin. Too thin.

"You scare me, Page, because when I look at you, I see myself. You know, we're not so different. I grew up in this town with an alcoholic dad who left me and my mom. And we had nothing. I always felt like a misfit. I couldn't afford to do the things other kids did. My mom used to take me to Seal Cove to shop in the thrift store, and I used to die in fear that someone from school would see me coming out of that shop with second-hand clothes. I spent all my teen years trying to prove that I wasn't just poor white trash." She looked down. "In some ways, I'm still trying…"

There was a long silence. Kestra leaned her head back and stared up at the ceiling. Why was she telling Page all this? She had never told anyone about shopping at the thrift store before, but suddenly it had become so fresh in her mind, as if it were yesterday. Kestra looked back down. A single tear streaked down Page's cheek.

"Do you want the job, Page?"

She nodded.

"Can you work on weekends until school is out?"

Again she nodded.

"Do you want to start today?"

Page smiled. It was a tiny smile. A small upturning of the corners of her mouth, something easily overlooked. But Kestra was sure that she wasn't mistaken.

~ 20 ~

Two weeks had flown by since Kestra had hired Page. And it had not been a mistake. Page showed herself to be a hard and willing worker. She followed directions carefully and tried very hard to please Kestra. Dan, as could be expected, gave Kestra a bad time at first, telling her she'd lost her senses to bring in a juvenile delinquent to work. But in time, even Dan changed his tune. And at Bible study, Karen thanked her profusely—for the third or fourth time.

"Karen, I should thank *you*," said Kestra as she picked up a piece of blueberry cheesecake. "Page is my right-hand gal. I can't wait until school's out and I can have her full time." She took a bite of the dessert, taking a moment to savor the creamy texture and flavor. "Holly," she called over her shoulder. "This cheesecake is totally amazing! You may have to abandon your business and come cook for me at The Wise Man's House after all!"

"Sorry, I can't take the credit," Holly replied as she carried in the coffeepot. "Karen made it. Isn't it heavenly?" Soon the rest of the small fellowship were all raving about it as well.

"Maybe we should make Karen head of Bible Study refreshments from now on," teased Matthew.

Holly threw a towel at him. "And just for that, you will be head of the clean-up crew!"

Kestra turned to Karen who was blushing with pride. "Karen, this is really good! Where'd you learn to cook like this?"

"I went to a culinary academy before I got married. And I was head chef for a couple years at Marcello's in Seattle. But then Page came along, and I wanted to be home..."

"You're kidding. You were head chef at Marcello's?"

"Well, that was a long time ago..."

"Where are you working now?"

"Actually, I just got a temporary job working for the school district. I'm a cook at the elementary school. Not exactly Marcello's, but they're talking about hiring me for next fall."

"I don't suppose you cook cheesecake for them."

Karen laughed. "Not hardly. But I have something lined up this summer at Seal Cove Resort, although I don't look forward to the long drives. I've even thought of moving up there if it all works out. But I must admit, I hate to move Page again, especially since she's so happy to be working for you. She's almost turning back into the old Page again."

"Karen, obviously I can't promise you much, but I think we should talk. You know I'll be looking for a chef, hopefully in the not-too-distant future. Do you think you'd possibly be up for it? I realize it's been a long time..."

Karen's eyes lit up. "Are you serious? Would you consider me? I could take more classes—or maybe if I worked real hard at Seal Cove I could get up to speed on the latest culinary trends. I just wouldn't want to disappoint you."

"Yes, I'm definitely interested. It's just that I'm not really sure when we'll open. Hopefully by midsummer. I'd suggest you go ahead with Seal Cove for now. But we'll have to keep talking and planning."

"Thank you, Kestra. You keep on giving me hope. It's almost as if God sent you for me."

Kestra threw her head back and laughed. "Are you sure it's not the other way around?"

The next day, Kestra began packing up her things from the cottage. Page came over, as usual, right after school.

"Kestra, tell me about this guy who's going to live here. Is he an old friend of yours or something?"

"No, actually, I only met Quin last winter. But we seemed to hit it right off. In fact, he used to live right here." She looked around the cottage in disbelief. It seemed like so much had happened since then.

"You seem real excited about him. Is there some romantic interest here?"

By now, Kestra was used to how Page cut straight to the point. And she appreciated her frankness. "I don't really know. I went out with Quin just before he left. I had a lovely time. And I must admit there's something very attractive about him. But I don't really know him that well. He isn't exactly the kind of guy to spill his guts, if you know what I mean."

"I didn't think most guys liked to spill their guts," laughed Page as she carefully wrapped a vase in a dishtowel.

"Well, I guess that's not exactly what I meant. He just doesn't talk about himself much. But I hope when he's living here I'll get to spend more time with him. Maybe I'll get to know him better. Then who knows…"

"Sounds romantic."

"Uh-huh. So, ready to take this load over?"

"Sure. Where are we going to put these kitchen things, since your kitchen isn't ready yet?"

"I plan to use the bedroom across the hall from my bedroom. I have a big old buffet I'll set up as a make-shift kitchen counter. I'll put a little microwave and hot plate on it, store dishes and what-not inside. I even bought a little fridge to use temporarily, and I'll bring in a table and chairs and—voila!"

"Sounds pretty fancy for a make-shift kitchen. What about water?"

"I guess I'll have to pretend like it's the old days and haul my own from the bathroom. Or else I can use a lot of disposable things. Although I prefer to eat off real dishes. I'll just have to wait and see how long it takes Dan to get the big kitchen in operation. Or maybe I'll have to have him put in a smaller one for personal use."

"Does Quin know how much trouble you're going through just so he can get in here?"

"No, and I don't want him to know. Understand?"

"My lips are sealed."

By the weekend, Kestra and Page had moved all her personal belongings from the cottage to the house. On Saturday afternoon, she took one final look around to make sure everything was perfect and in its place. She considered leaving fresh flowers on the table, but she wasn't exactly sure which day he was coming. Besides, she didn't want to appear overly anxious.

All the furnishings and anything Quin might need were here. She wanted him to be completely comfortable. Besides, the last time he had stayed here it had been furnished. Certainly nothing like this though. She smiled as she remembered his appreciation for the way she and Holly had fixed it up. She hoped he would enjoy it.

It was her first night to sleep in her bedroom in the Wise Man's House. It was so spacious compared to the cottage that at first she felt nearly lost in it. But she turned on her stereo and let the floating sounds of Bach fill the room as she enjoyed a long luxurious bath in the oversized clawfoot tub. Yes, she'd been right to get in here. It was wonderful!

As she towel-dried her hair, she admired the sheen of the

rosewood four-poster bed, recently refinished by her own two hands. It was adorned in a fluffy white Battenburg lace duvet cover with matching pillows and dust-ruffle. It looked like a bed fit for a princess. Or even a perfect honeymoon suite! For a moment she imagined sharing this room with a husband. The only face that could come into her imagination was that of Quin. Even the thought of him made her heart flutter. Could it be possible that he might be back in Port Star by tomorrow? Although he'd said June, he'd never actually said June first. Perhaps she was being ridiculous. She had to stop allowing her imagination to run wild like this.

She started to reach for her flannel nightshirt hanging on a hook in her closet. Then she spotted a white silky gown on top of a box not yet unpacked. She lifted it up. It smelled of the lavender sachets that she had used in her drawers. This was a gown more fitting for a princess! She slipped it on and briefly waltzed to the music, floating barefoot across the smooth wood floor. She remembered the last time she had danced, the feel of his hand, the tilt of his chin… She had to put a stop to this daydreaming; she was getting too swept away in her fantasy. She knew it was possible to fall in love with an illusion. She also knew it was dangerous.

Just as she was about to crawl in bed, Riley looked up with soft brown eyes. By now, he was used to sleeping on her bed, but this new four-poster was different, and it was taller. She looked at the pure white bed linen then back at Riley.

"Just one night in your own bed, okay, Riley?" she asked. "Can't I just for one night sleep like a princess?" He cocked his head to one side as if trying to decipher her words. She scooted his seldom-used dog bed right next to her bed and patted the soft plaid cushion. "There you go, boy. Get in your bed, now. I'll be right here." He looked up with melt-your-heart eyes as she climbed into bed, but she was determined to ignore him.

She turned off the light and lay back against the soft pillow.

Riley tossed and turned in his bed as if it were a bed of nails. Finally he began to whine like a small child. She turned on the light and climbed out of bed, rummaging through the linen closet until she found an old stadium blanket. She spread it across the foot of her bed, then patted it. "Here boy," she said. He hopped right up and gave her his best doggy smile.

"So much for being a princess," she said as she snapped off the light. "Good night, my sweet little prince."

The next morning, pure light gleamed in the window with the promise of a beautiful day. She pulled back the curtains and looked out over the sea. It glistened as if the touch of the sun had stirred it back to life. After the past few days of heavy fog this was most welcome—and perfect for the first day of June! She looked back to her bed to discover that Riley had sneaked off his blanket and snuggled in the spot next to hers sometime in the night. There was now a smudge of gray on the white Battenburg lace. She'd have to look into another style of bedding next week. White and Riley just would not mix.

She pulled on her robe and walked across the hall to her temporary kitchen. Last night, she'd carried in a jug of water, and this she used to fill the coffeemaker. She ground the beans and listened to the whirring sound echo through the empty house. She filled the filter and turned on the coffeemaker. This wasn't so bad. Since she'd agreed to meet Holly for breakfast before church, she would not need to worry about cooking.

She dressed for church, keeping in mind that there was just the slightest possibility that she might see Quin today. She knew that Faith Fellowship was much more casual than Dan's church. Some women even wore jeans, but she wasn't quite comfortable with that. Still, she didn't want to overdress. Today she chose a straight denim skirt which she topped with a butter-yellow sweater set. It seemed like something that Quin might like—just in case. She carefully styled her hair in a thick french braid, letting it trail down her back, clamped with a small tortoise-shell barrette. She took her cup of coffee outside as she watched Riley romp and enjoy the fresh spring air. He dashed over to the steps that led to the beach and looked back at her expectantly.

"Not right now, boy. We'll do that later." She wished Riley's dog run were installed. The landscape designer had worked a discreet one into a corner by the stable, and with sunny weather coming she longed to provide a safe place for him to be during the day when she wasn't around. Just as she put Riley back in the house, she heard a vehicle pull up. She turned quickly to see. Could it possibly be him? With disappointment she recognized the pickup.

"Hi, Kestra," called Dan as he stepped from his truck. She looked at him curiously. Had he actually come to work on a Sunday? But when he stepped around she could see that he wasn't dressed for work.

"What's up, Dan?" she asked suspiciously.

"I saw Matthew and Holly last night, and Matthew invited me to church. At first, I said no, but then Matthew suggested I might come with you and Holly. So here I am. Actually, Holly told me you two were having breakfast at eight. So I thought I could join you. Hope you don't mind. My treat!" He smiled, and somehow it reminded her of Riley's pleading last night. As much as she wanted to, how could she say no? What kind of Christian turned her back on a person who wanted to go to church?

She shrugged. "Sure, maybe we should both drive and meet Holly in town."

"Nah, I'll drive. I don't mind bringing you back." Before she could say no, he opened the passenger side of his pickup. To her surprise it was clean inside.

"So how was the first night?" asked Dan. "Did you sleep

okay? It seems kind of big and lonely in that old house. Did you get scared at all?"

She laughed. "No, I slept just fine, thank you. I've got Riley for company. And besides, I believe that God is watching out for me."

Holly looked surprised when Kestra walked into the restaurant with Dan. "Looks like there'll be three of us," she said to the waitress.

Kestra threw her a look that said this wasn't her idea. "Dan told me how you and Matthew invited him to come to church with us today. And he thought it would be fun to join us for breakfast, too."

"My treat," he said again. "And I must say what a pleasure it is to dine with such lovely ladies."

"Uh-huh," murmured Kestra as she studied the menu. She had been looking forward to chatting with Holly about the fact that Quin might be here today. Now she wouldn't bring it up.

After church Matthew offered to take Holly home, and Dan and Kestra drove back to Port Star alone in his pickup. Actually this was preferable to being wedged between Dan and Holly like on the way over. She felt fairly certain that he had planned the whole thing just so he could rub shoulders with her, probably hoping to make some sparks. But even if he could make sparks, they weren't the kind she was interested in. She remembered those sparks as the kind that could hurt and burn.

In fact, that torturously long drive had almost ruined the church service for her. Almost. Fortunately, she was able to tune out the fact that Dan Hackett was sitting next to her during the service and focus on God instead. By the time the service ended she was refreshed. Now if she could just survive the forty-minute drive back.

"So what do you think of Faith Fellowship, Dan?" she asked, hoping to keep the conversation in comfortable territory.

"It was okay, I guess. Pretty different from St. Johns. They sure do sing a lot there."

She laughed. "Yep, they sure do."

"You seemed to really like it."

"I do like it. I feel like I belong there."

"I think I'd like to come back and try it again."

She nodded without looking at him. She was glad for him, but she hoped he wasn't doing it for her sake. He flipped on the radio to a country station, and they rode in silence for a long while. Then finally, about a mile from her house, he turned off the radio.

"You know, Kestra, I can change."

"Change? What do you mean?"

"Well, I know I've made some mistakes. And I know I'm not really that religious, but I can change. I can do better."

She almost wanted to laugh. He sounded like a little kid promising not to steal candy anymore. But she could tell by his face that he was perfectly serious. Why was he telling her this? Did he think she wanted him to change?

"Anyone can change, Dan. But unless God's doing the changing, it might not make a whole lot of difference."

He frowned as if he didn't quite get it. At last, he turned down her driveway. She quickly glanced over to the cottage but couldn't see any sign of Quin yet. Of course, he could have parked on the other side.

"Thanks for the ride, Dan," she said lightly as she stepped down from the pickup, eager to escape his company. To her disappointment, he turned off the engine and got out, too.

"I just don't know what you want from me, Kestra."

She started to say she didn't want anything from him, but she saw someone approaching from the corner of her eye. She turned to see Quin walking toward them. He was here! Really here. It took every ounce of self control not to jump up and down like a preschooler.

She waved to Quin, doubly glad to terminate this conversation with Dan. "Hi, Quin!"

Dan turned and looked, too. She noticed his eyes following Quin the whole time, almost like a predator might watch his prey. When Dan turned back to Kestra, his face was dark and cloudy.

"Quin, you remember Dan Hackett," she spoke with a slight tremor in her voice. She hoped they didn't notice. "Dan, you already met Quin Larson. He's the new tenant of the cottage."

Quin extended his hand. Dan hesitated just for a split second, but long enough to communicate something. Kestra wasn't exactly sure what that was, but she didn't like it.

"You'll recall Dan is my contractor," said Kestra to Quin.

"And long time friend," added Dan patting her on the back. "Not to mention high school sweetheart. Right, Kestra?" He laughed, but it wasn't a genuine laugh. Why was he acting like this? All along she had made her feelings clear.

"Well, I gotta go. I'll see you in the morning, Kestra." Dan climbed into the pickup and pulled out quickly. Too quickly. She knew he was angry and it embarrassed her that he acted so childish.

"Everything okay?" asked Quin. His eyes looked concerned and even a little curious. "Did I come at a bad time?"

"No. It's just that Dan Hackett can't seem to take a hint!" Her cheeks were hot now. She was embarrassed by her own anger. This was not anything like how she planned to welcome Quin back to the Wise Man's House. Why was it that Dan Hackett always seemed to get the best of her?

～ 21 ～

hen did you get here?" Kestra asked as she walked Quin back to the cottage.

"Just a few minutes ago. I wasn't sure if I should let myself in or wait for you."

"Oh, it would have been fine to go in. It's all ready for you. It's not locked or anything. I stuck a key under the flowerpot. I'll show you."

"It's such a nice day, I figured you might be out on the beach since your car was here."

"I went to church. Dan drove." She wanted to explain that she hadn't wanted to go with Dan, but didn't know how to without making it sound ridiculous.

"I'll just grab some things on my way in," said Quin. Kestra stepped onto the small porch and opened the door, waiting. She watched as he walked up carrying what looked like a heavy box loaded with books. She liked the way his long legs seemed to swing from the hips in one smooth motion. He carried the box with ease, slipping past her as she held the screen door open. His denim shirt sleeve brushed against her as he went by, giving her a sensation that made her blush.

"I put in a bookshelf over here," she pointed to the stacked lawyers bookcase by the fireplace. The front of the glass still shone from her recent cleaning spree.

"Hey, great! Last time I was here I just kept my books stacked on the floor." He set down the box, then stood and looked at her. She suddenly remembered the night they had danced, and once again she was flooded with feelings and longings that she was afraid might be written all over her face. She turned her attention back to the bookcase.

"Can I help you put these books away?"

"Sure, I'll get the rest of my stuff."

"Do you like them in any certain order?"

He laughed. "No, I'm not too particular. Thanks."

She knelt down and began picking books from the box and placing them on the shelf. At first she was too rattled to notice the titles, but at last she calmed down and realized this was a perfect chance to learn a little something about him. Jack used to say you couldn't judge a book by a cover, but you could judge a man by a book. She wasn't sure if that was really true, but it might not hurt to keep it in mind.

Many of the books were old classics, titles she'd heard of but had never actually read. Somehow this didn't surprise her, Quin seemed like the literary type. She wondered if she could even relate to him on an intellectual level. What if he thought she was some sort of fluff head? She was relieved to see a smattering of contemporary novels and bestsellers, some she had read, some she had wanted to. Maybe that would give her an excuse for an occasional visit, to borrow a book. She was getting to the bottom of the box when Quin finally brought in his last load.

"That's it!" he announced.

She glanced at the suitcases and boxes and crates near the door. "You sure travel light. Is that really all your worldly possessions?"

He laughed. "Pretty much. About a year ago, I decided to streamline my life. I'd been feeling pretty entangled and even trapped. I wanted to get free from things. I was feeling more and more like my things owned me, more than I owned them."

She turned back to the nearly empty book box. What must he think of her? Here she seemed to be stockpiling all kinds of things for The Wise Man's House. Of course, that was going to be her livelihood, and she needed those things to make it work. Maybe that made it different. She pulled a familiar-looking book from the box. It was a recently released Patrick O'Riley novel. She started to say something, then noticed there were more. She pulled out one after the next. He had every single edition, and they seemed to be brand new, never cracked open.

"Quin!" she stood with a handful of books, almost as if she'd caught him with some sort of contraband. "You didn't tell me you liked Patrick O'Riley. Don't you remember when I told you about who I named my dog after?"

He grinned a lop-sided grin. "Just who said I like O'Riley anyway?"

She walked into the kitchen where he was unloading a bag of groceries and waved several titles in his face. "So if you don't like him, why do you have all his books?" Suddenly she wondered if he might have gotten them simply because she had mentioned loving this author. That could easily explain why they were all unread. How sweet to think he might have done that for her.

"Just because I have his books doesn't mean I like him."

"So then why would you buy all his books?"

"Who said I bought them?" He grinned again. But when she noticed those sweet tiny creases by the corners of his eyes she knew she was beat. She threw up her hands and surrendered.

"Are you always this impossible?"

"Sometimes I'm even worse!"

She returned to the bookcase and carefully placed the O'Riley books in order. There were sixteen of them, all neat and in a row.

"Thanks, you do nice work," said Quin, coming into the living room. He stretched out a hand and helped her rise to her feet. "Now as a thank you, can I make you some lunch, or did you and Dan already eat?"

She wanted to say 'Dan means nothing to me!' but instead she said, "That sounds like a pretty good deal. Is there anything else I can help you unpack?" She looked toward his other boxes. She was curious about what was inside.

"No, there's not much there. Why don't you just sit down and tell me how the house is coming? By the way, do you like BLTs?"

"Sounds scrumptious!" She leaned against the counter and watched as he reached for the frying pan that was hanging above the stove and laid out several strips of bacon.

"So did that copper ceiling get installed yet?" he asked as he sliced thick slices of tomato.

"Yes, and it looks fabulous. Why don't you come see it after lunch?" She watched as he carefully laid out slices of bread and spread them with mayonnaise. "It looks like you know your way around a kitchen." She tried to make it sound like a compliment, but it wasn't from the heart.

"Does that bother you?" He turned and looked her right in the eye. She glanced away uncomfortably.

"No, not really…"

"Actually, the only things I can make are BLTs, cheese omelets, and hotcakes. And I brew a pretty mean cup of coffee."

She smiled. "I know it's silly, but my husband was such a terrific cook that I never really got very confident in the kitchen. And his standards were so high…"

"Jack?"

"Yes, you remembered his name."

He nodded as he laid dark green lettuce leaves on top of the bread. "It seems a little odd that you're planning to open a restaurant if you feel that way about cooking."

She laughed. "Well, I don't plan to cook. Although, I'm not all that bad, and since I moved down here I've been getting better with practice. But I do understand what makes good food and good presentation. I learned a lot about running a restaurant from Jack."

He set the sandwiches on plates and placed them on the table. "Well, I hope this makes good food. I don't know about the presentation. Is orange juice okay with it? Or would that fight with the tomato?"

She knew he was teasing, but she didn't mind. It wasn't like it had been with Jack. "Orange juice is just fine."

He sat down and looked at her, but she didn't move. "Do you normally pray before you eat?"

She shrugged her shoulders, not knowing what to say. "Not normally, but my norms seem to be constantly changing these days."

She was both surprised and relieved when he bowed his head and said a simple prayer. Then he smiled. "Dig in!"

After lunch, Kestra showed him the progress on the house.

"The place is coming along fine," he said. He ran his hand over the smoke-darkened fireplace mantle in the library. "Any plans for restoring this?"

"Dan says it would be cheaper and easier to just replace it. See where it's split here? But I don't know…"

"Want me to take a hand at it?"

She looked at him in disbelief. "Do you actually do woodworking?"

"I've been known to do a little now and then. I find it very relaxing."

"Sort of like sketching?"

"In a bigger way."

"That would be great. I'd love to see it restored. Maybe I can deduct it from your rent. Do you want to see the upstairs now? There's still a lot to do."

"Sure, then I'd like to go for a walk while the sun's still out. I noticed a fog bank off on the horizon."

She pointed out the new flooring and some of the work that was in progress in some of the spare bedrooms. Then she showed him her temporary kitchen.

"It's a little crude, but I don't mind. In fact, I kind of like the old-fashioned feeling of making do."

"I didn't rush you to get moved into this house before you were ready, did I?" He looked around the make-shift set up.

"No, no, not at all. I was eager to get in here. For one thing, the bedroom in the cottage was feeling a little cramped, and I wanted more closet space." She spoke quickly, not wanting him to feel guilty. "Come see how much nicer my bedroom is now." She opened the door to her room, then wondered how that might seem. "I mean, it's just so much roomier, and what with the lovely view and all..." Suddenly she was painfully aware that they were together in a rather intimate setting—a place that just last night she had dreamed of sharing. Her cheeks blazed with the memory, and she could think of nothing more to say. She was relieved to see Riley romp in and didn't even mind when he flopped both dusty paws on the front of her skirt.

"This is beautiful, Kestra. You really have a knack for making a place look nice." He stepped over to the window, and she tried to relax. It didn't seem to bother him that they were alone in her bedroom. "Terrific view. It must be nice to see the sun set from up here."

She stood beside him with one hand on Riley's head and

gazed out the window. "Yes, it is. So you see, I didn't really give up anything to move over here."

He turned to her and looked down into her face for a long moment. Her heart was pounding and for the second time, she thought he might kiss her. But then he turned back to the window.

"Well, I'd like to get some fresh air. Do you and Riley want to join me?" He reached down and patted Riley's shiny head. "You are quite a handsome fellow, ol' boy," he said as he continued to stroke his sleek coat. "Want to go for a walk?"

Riley's tail wagged as if he understood.

"I guess that's your answer," laughed Kestra. "Maybe you and Riley can head down, while I get into some walking clothes."

"Come on, boy," called Quin, slapping his leg. To Kestra's surprise, Riley followed. So much for loyalty. Still, she was glad that Riley liked Quin, too.

She quickly pulled on jeans and her fisherman-knit sweater. Although it was sunny, it still wasn't all that warm on the beach. She looked at her face in the mirror. She wasn't surprised to see the glow of pink on her cheeks. At least it wasn't the cherry red that she'd imagined. And it really didn't look that bad. She skipped down the stairs and found Quin and Riley waiting out in front.

The three of them romped on the beach for a couple of hours, tossing the stick for Riley and racing back and forth like children. Kestra had never felt so good! She had never felt so alive! If this wasn't true love, she couldn't imagine anything better.

Finally, they headed back home. After all their laughing and joking on the beach, she felt comfortable with him. That feeling of anticipation was almost gone. But the magic was still there. At the top of the beach stairs they paused, both pointed in different directions. Then Quin joined her in walking back toward the house.

"It's so good to be back here, Kestra. I can't tell you how glad I am to be settled back into the cottage. I want you to know how much I appreciate—"

Quin stopped as the pickup pulled into view. It was Dan, but Kestra couldn't imagine what he had come for. As he pulled closer she noticed Holly sitting next to him. She hoped nothing was wrong.

"Hey, Kestra," he called as he stepped out. "You ready?"

"For what?"

"Church. Remember, this is church night." Dan said it like they had some kind of agreement. She couldn't remember setting anything like this up.

Holly jumped down from the pickup. "Dan said we might as well all go to church together tonight." She gave Kestra a questioning look, as if she suspected something was amiss. She glanced curiously at Quin, then back over to Dan.

"I'm sorry, you've just taken me by surprise," said Kestra. "Holly, this is Quin Larson. Quin, this is Holly Vincent, my best friend." She grabbed Holly by the arm and guided her to the front porch. "Come here, best friend," she whispered. "What is going on here, Holly? Are you guys trying to bushwhack me, or have I just lost my marbles and nobody wants to tell me?"

"Dan said you wanted the three of us to go to church together tonight," Holly whispered helplessly. "That's all I know. And you must admit, it's nice that Dan is so interested in church."

"Sure, if that's what he's interested in." Kestra glanced over to the driveway. Dan was talking to Quin. No telling what he might be saying. She hurried over to see if she could clear things up.

"I'd invite you to come, Quin," said Dan loudly. "But you can see it would be a mite bit crowded, what with the two ladies and all. Although it could be cozy." He grinned at Kestra and she wanted to punch him.

"Actually, I'm not sure I'm going tonight." She met Dan's gaze with narrowed eyes, then smiled. "So if Quin would like to go in my place—"

Dan opened his mouth to protest, but Quin spoke first.

"No, thanks, you folks go on along. I've had a long day, and I still have some unpacking to do. Thanks for the walk, Kestra." Quin began walking away. She wanted to cry out, wanted to tell him that Dan was being a manipulative jerk, but instead she turned and glared at Dan.

"Don't you want to come to church with us, Kestra?" he smiled hopefully. "Holly said the evening service is pretty casual. You probably don't even need to change. Come on, I'm sorry if I caught you by surprise, but you gave me the impression that you wanted to go to this church on a regular basis. And all day I've been thinking about some things that preacher said. I want to go back and see if this is really for real."

Maybe she was just being a horrible ogre. Maybe she should just hop in and go with them. Kestra looked at Holly for advice.

"Come on, Kestra," encouraged Holly.

Kestra faced Holly so Dan couldn't see her and spoke quietly. "If I come, will you promise to ride back with us? No abandoning me with him this time?"

Holly nodded. "We better get going."

"Let me put Riley away." She took the dog in the house and wondered if she would always be such a pushover. When she came back out, Holly was climbing into the passenger's side and scooting to the middle, obviously trying to spare Kestra from being wedged in the middle again. Kestra said a silent blessing on her friend. But before Kestra could climb in after Holly, Dan shut the door and took her arm.

"Here, you can get in on my side, Kestra." She was so surprised that she could think of nothing to say, and allowed herself to be led to the driver's side of the truck. She slipped in and sat dumbly in the middle, turning to make a puckered face to Holly. Holly gave an apologetic smile, and Kestra swore she would never let Dan Hackett best her again. As they pulled around the driveway she saw Quin in back of the cottage breaking down empty boxes. He looked up and watched as they drove away.

She had a very difficult time paying attention during the worship service, but she did have a chance to ask God to soften her heart toward Dan. Or at least to help her not to kill him.

22

O kay, I want the whole scoop, Kestra," said Holly in a confidential tone as they basked in the sunlight of a Saturday afternoon. "It's been two weeks since Quin arrived, and I've hardly seen hide nor hair of you. I even arranged for Mom to mind the shop today just so I could come out here and get the whole story."

"Well, it's not like you aren't fairly caught up in something of a romance of your own, Holly." Kestra stretched her legs out before her and leaned back into the chaise lounge. She had finally broken down and purchased some decent patio furniture. "In fact, if you remember correctly, I did call you last week. I even left a message on your machine—"

"Yeah, yeah. I know. But let's get to the good stuff. What's going on? You haven't been to church or Bible study since he came. Is he leading you astray or something?"

Kestra laughed. "No, of course not! It's just, the only time I get to visit with him is in the evenings, so it was hard to give up the last two Wednesdays. But I plan on coming back soon, maybe even tomorrow."

"Good. The group is missing you. Besides that, it's been getting pretty interesting since Dan began coming—"

"You're kidding!"

"No, he's been there the last two times, although he was a bit miffed that you weren't there. I'm surprised he didn't come over and take you against your will."

"Well, I've been sort of avoiding him…"

"How exactly do you avoid a man who is working in your house every day?"

"Actually, he hasn't been here too much lately. Which I'm finding pretty aggravating. Things seem to be moving pretty slowly right now."

"Maybe he's punishing you."

"What an awful thought. Do you really think so?"

"No, that wasn't a very nice thing for me to say. Actually, I think old Danny Boy might be turning over a new leaf. He seems to be getting interested in knowing more about the Bible. He even had a couple of theological discussions with Matthew."

"Do you think he's sincere about all this?" Kestra hated the suspicious tone of her voice, but it was so hard to believe Dan was serious.

"How can anyone make that kind of judgment? Now remember, I didn't come over here to discuss Dan's spiritual development. Tell me all about this mystery man. Did you know that Dan calls him the vampire?"

"The vampire!" Kestra sat up and stared at Holly in disbelief. "You've got to be kidding! What does he mean by that?"

"He says that Quin never shows his face during the daylight hours, he only comes out at night."

"Can you blame him with Dan around?"

Holly laughed and took a drink of soda. "So what does he do all day? Is he self-employed or something?"

"I guess so…"

"What do you mean you 'guess so'? Don't you know by now? It's been weeks!"

Kestra shrugged, then glanced over her shoulder.

"Expecting someone?"

"I just like to keep an eye out for Dan. I don't really want him eavesdropping. He's taken a dislike to Quin, and I don't want him to pop in and hear me."

"I thought he was gone for the day."

"It's his style to drop in unexpectedly. I almost get the feeling he plans it to catch me off guard. But I'm probably just being paranoid."

Holly nodded and grinned. "So back to the subject. What exactly do you know about this Quin guy anyway—if that's really his name."

"What do you mean?"

"Well, Dan has some suspicions. He even shared with our Bible study that he was concerned about you. He thinks Quin might be something of a shady character."

Kestra shook her head. "If that doesn't just take the cake!"

"Well, you don't seem to know much about him yourself."

"I know he's a good guy."

"Then explain why no one, including yourself, knows what he does for a living. And why does he live in a little caretaker's cottage, but he drives a rig that only lawyers, doctors, or crooks can normally afford. And you said yourself that he only brought a few things with him. And what does he do all day in there?"

Put in that sort of way, Kestra could see how it might look a little strange. "Maybe he's just eccentric. I don't know…"

"Well, what do you guys talk about? Does he tell you about his past?"

"No, not really. I've told him just about everything there is to know about me. He's a good listener, and occasionally he offers a bit of sound advice, but not in a pushy way. He's really quite comfortable to be with. In fact, talking with him has really

176

helped me to accept some of the things from my past."

"So he's a psychologist? A therapist?"

"I don't know. Maybe. He's just very wise."

Holly sighed. "I hope for your sake that this guy is on the level."

Kestra was getting irritated now. Holly might be her best friend, but there were limits. Just because Quin wasn't the perfect Christian leader that Matthew seemed to be was no reason to get all suspicious. "So what do you think he's into, Holly? Maybe he manufactures drugs, or maybe he's an ax murderer hiding from the law. Or maybe he's a vampire!"

Holly laughed. "I'm sorry, Kestra. I just worry about you out here all by yourself. And you must admit, you haven't given me a chance to get to know him. Even Matthew is a little concerned."

"I think Dan Hackett has been poisoning everyone's mind against Quin. I'll tell you what, how about if I have you and Matthew over for dinner, and you can get to know Quin for yourselves. And you know what else, I'll even invite him to church or Bible study. I do happen to know that he's a Christian, if that makes you feel any better. He seems very quiet about his faith, but I am positive that it's genuine. I can tell by the way he treats me."

"I'm sure you know what you're into, Kestra. And you may be right about Dan. It's plain that he's as jealous as the dickens. But I'll hold you to the dinner invite. Speaking of food, I want to see that kitchen. Dan said all your fancy kitchen things just arrived from Portland. It sounds like he's not too excited about installing them though."

Kestra groaned. "Yes, he's made it very clear that this is a great inconvenience to him. But I think if he put as much energy into doing it as he does fussing about it, the kitchen would be all done. Anyway, come see." She led Holly into the house. "As far as I can tell, everything's ready to go into place. I don't know why Dan's dragging his heels so much. But I really suspect it might have something to do with Quin."

"So, do you have a projected finish date? Didn't you want to open the restaurant while it was still summer?"

"I'm still hoping for that. At one time, Dan had promised by early July. But the rate he's going now, I don't know…"

"Hmm, it doesn't really look like there's too much more to do. Maybe it could be finished in a few weeks."

They walked through the house, and Holly admired everything all over again. Her enthusiasm bolstered Kestra's spirits. It really had come a long way. Maybe the end wasn't too far off after all.

"You know, Kestra, I have an ulterior motive for wanting this house done soon."

"What's that?" asked Kestra as she opened a crate and pulled out a nice white china plate trimmed in gold and dark green. "These are for the restaurant."

Holly took the plate and nodded. "Yes, those would be perfect for what I have in mind."

"What's that?" asked Kestra.

"Perfect for a wedding reception. Can't you just imagine the bride coming down the staircase, and—"

"You mean you and Matthew?" Kestra grabbed Holly's arm and let out a happy shriek.

"Well, he hasn't actually asked, but I think it might happen."

"That is so cool, Holly! And here we've been talking about me. Tell me everything. This is great! And of course, you must have the wedding here! How about August or maybe September?"

Holly laughed. "Now, hold on there, girl. That might be pushing things just a little too fast. The groom doesn't even know about the wedding yet."

"Of course. But maybe we could have some wingding of an engagement party!" She carefully wrapped the dish back in bubble paper and placed it in the box. "You know, Christmas weddings are nice, too…"

They spent the rest of the afternoon chattering about what sort of wedding it might be, how they would decorate, what the cake would be like, and where the happy couple might live after their honeymoon in the Bahamas.

"Hey, Kestra!" called Page from the back of the house.

"In the library," answered Kestra.

"How's Page doing these days?" asked Holly quietly.

"Shh." Kestra jabbed her gently with an elbow. Page walked in. She was wearing loose-fitting overalls and had a streak of dark green paint across one cheek.

"Hey, Page, how's it coming?" asked Kestra. "I'm sorry, I was going to come out and help you paint that trim on the stable. How does that color look?"

"It looks pretty good, I think. And I'm all done."

"Hi, Page," said Holly. "You can blame me for distracting Kestra from her work."

"Yes, here we are planning weddings, and you're out there sweating it out."

"Weddings?" Page's brows shot up and Holly elbowed Kestra.

"Well, not for real. No one's really engaged or anything," Kestra glanced nervously at Holly. "It's okay, Holly, Page can be trusted. Can't you, Page? She knows all kinds of secrets about me, and as far as I know they haven't made it into town."

Page grinned. "Yeah, but you pay me."

Kestra pretended to punch her. "Hey, why don't you go grab a soda. You look pretty parched. Then you can show me how the stable looks. Want to come out and see it, Holly?"

"Sure, but why are you working on the stable, Kestra?

You're not planning to get a horse are you?"

Kestra laughed. "No, I just wanted it to look nice. See, it's visible from the south wing, and I want that to be the major dining area. Only I want to add a whole bunch of windows all the way around, kind of like a sun room."

"And besides, it's so cool out there," said Page. "I really like working in the stable. I wouldn't mind living in it, I mean if it was more fixed up or something." Page glanced down at her feet.

"It looks good, Page," said Kestra. "You did more than just paint." Everything was swept clean, and Page had even pulled out the overgrown grass and weeds that had grown between the brick path that went all around the outside of the stable.

Holly peeked into a stall. "All that's missing is the horse."

"We used to have horses," said Page sadly.

"I didn't know that," said Kestra. "What kind?"

"My mom had a couple of Arabian mares. She was hoping to get them bred and start a little business. But she had to sell them when we moved."

"That's too bad," said Holly. "Do you miss them?"

Page didn't answer.

Holly glanced at her watch. "Oh, no, I almost forgot, I'm supposed to meet Matthew at the shop at five. I have to run. Thanks for the visit, Kestra. Do you need a ride into town, Page?"

Page tipped her head to the old Ford parked by the stable. "Thanks anyway. I'm driving the Beemer today." Holly laughed and waved good-bye.

Page scraped the toe of her shoe through the dirt. "I found some old tack in one of the stalls. It's probably not good for anything, but it's kind of interesting. Want to see?"

"Sure. I suppose it might be collectable."

"I thought you might want to hang some of it on the inside

walls here, sort of like decoration, you know." She picked up an old leather yoke and what looked like a buggy whip.

"Page, that's a brilliant idea! Do you want to take a stab at it? You know, I eventually hope to get the grounds all fixed up with trails and benches so that guests can enjoy a little before-dinner or after-dinner walk. I even thought about putting in a pond over there." She pointed between the house and the stable. "Maybe a gazebo, too."

"Hello, there," called a familiar voice.

"Hi, Quin, we're back here," answered Kestra. "Come join our planning party!"

"Not weddings this time," whispered Page, and Kestra giggled.

"Hey, this looks nice," said Quin as he inspected the stable.

"Thanks to Page." Kestra patted her on the back. It was so fun to see Page smile. And it seemed to happen more and more. "And then Page came up with this great idea to hang this neat old tack around to decorate."

Quin nodded. "It almost seems a shame to let this nice stable go empty. You know, there was a time not so long ago when folks couldn't survive without horses." He ran his hand along a post that had been worn smooth, probably by animals going in and out.

"I wish I could afford to buy a horse and keep it here," said Page wistfully. Kestra looked at Quin. Her instinct was to say 'why not?' But then again, it wasn't as if Page were her own child.

"I wouldn't mind having a horse myself," said Quin.

"Really?" Page's eyes lit up. "I could take care of it for you. I know a lot about horses. I mean, if it was okay. I mean, if Kestra would let you—"

Kestra laughed. "He's a grown man. Why would he need to ask me if he could have a horse?"

"Well, I mean, I assumed he'd keep it here…" Page looked flustered as if she'd stuck her foot in her mouth.

"Of course he could keep it here if he wanted. In fact, who knows, maybe I'd like a horse, too." Suddenly Kestra grabbed them both by the arm. "I've got it!"

"What?" asked Page. "What?"

"Why don't I get several horses? I could offer dinner and romantic horse rides on the beach! You know what I was saying about making this place really lovely with a pond and trails and benches. Why not offer horses, too? Wouldn't that be something!"

Quin scratched his beard. "You might just be on to something."

"Oh, Kestra, if you do, can I please, please, be your stable girl? I'll clean stalls. I'll feed and groom and anything you want—if I could only ride the horses, too."

"Of course, Page! I wouldn't have it any other way!"

"Thanks, Kestra." Page was smiling so widely that Kestra didn't even notice the pierced nose and multiple earrings. All she could see was a happy teenager who loved horses.

"It sounds like a pretty big plan," said Quin.

"I'm so excited!" gushed Page. "I wish I didn't have to go, but I need to get the car back to mom, she's working the dinner shift at Seal Cove. Bye, Kestra. Bye, Quin."

Kestra and Quin stood in front of the stable discussing what sort of horses might be best to get. Quin seemed to know a lot about horses, and Kestra knew nothing.

"Do you think you'd have time to help me pick out some good horses?" asked Kestra. She remembered what Holly had said about what he might do all day long.

"Sure, I'll pick up a paper tomorrow and check the classifieds. But before you get in too deep, you should realize there's a lot more to horses than just picking them out. Even if we find a good deal, they are not cheap to keep. You should never invest in horses to make money. In fact, it's best to just consider them a very expensive hobby."

"But couldn't I deduct them as a business expense?"

"My dear, you are a natural born businesswoman."

She smiled. Nothing he could have said would have meant more to her. Well, almost nothing.

❧ 23 ❧

D o you have any plans for dinner?" asked Kestra as she and Quin walked away from the stable.

"Not to speak of. I have a microwave meal in the freezer, but I wasn't looking forward to it."

"I picked up a couple of nice salmon fillets in town today, and I thought I might throw a salad together..." Kestra turned and smiled. Inviting a man to dinner felt strange to her, and more than a little awkward. Sure, she had packed them a couple of picnics to share on the beach, but she'd never actually asked him to join her for dinner in her own house. This felt like a big step in their relationship. Maybe it was premature on her part.

"I'd love it," he said. "Can I bring anything?"

"No, I've got everything. How about around seven?"

"Sounds perfect! And I have a surprise for you." His eyes twinkled and he gave a playful tug on her long french braid. She looked up with curiosity. What did he mean? But she wasn't ready to ask. She would make herself be patient and wait. Besides, she liked surprises.

"See you at seven, then," she called as she headed toward the house. Riley romped up and threw both paws on her, wagging his tail eagerly. Then he sprinted the few yards to Quin and did the same thing. It was his way of saying it was time for a walk.

"Sorry, boy." Quin patted his head. "We have things to do. Maybe we can take a walk after dinner." He looked at Kestra. "Is that okay with you?"

"Sounds great! Come on, Riley," She slapped her knee a couple of times and took off in a run toward the house with Riley quickly racing ahead. He met her at the door, tail thumping with pride.

"Yes, you are the fastest dog ever!" She stroked his head and opened the door. Life was good! How could things get any better? She looked around her half-finished house and didn't even mind that it was in such a partial state. She could live like this forever, with true love in her life—

Those two words stopped her in midstep halfway up the stairs. True love. Was she truly in love with Quin? All along she had assured herself that it was only infatuation, or maybe a crush that would wear off in time. She hadn't allowed herself to think about the possibility, or even the luxury, of real true love. That was too big, too overwhelming. And besides, she wasn't ready to think about it right now. It might mess things up. Better to leave things as they were. She walked slowly up the stairs, irritated at herself for even thinking about such things as 'true love.' She would put it out of her mind. At least for tonight.

"What will be, will be." She spoke out loud at the top of the landing. "And Lord, please take control of all this. You know what's best. You know what I need. As well as what I don't need."

She went into her make-shift kitchen and began carefully constructing a green salad. She had gotten all kinds of interesting produce from the organic grocery store in town. She had even discussed the possibility of having them supply her restaurant once it got started, and the owner had been very interested and full of helpful ideas. She arranged the colorful greens like the petals of a big flower, with slender slices of tomato, red onion, and mushroom in the center. She covered the salad with plastic wrap and proudly placed it in the tiny fridge right next to what looked like an asparagus bouquet. She had cut the tough ends off and stuck them in a jar of water, just the way Jack had always done. Later she would steam them whole. She didn't really like asparagus that much. But it had been Jack's favorite vegetable, and it seemed to go well with salmon. She had already told Quin that cooking was not her strong suit, but tonight she wanted to show him she wasn't helpless in the kitchen.

She ran downstairs and dug through boxes until she found candles and candleholders, a tablecloth, china, goblets, and silver. She piled all this into a basket and carried it upstairs. She wished she had a dining table set up downstairs, but she hadn't moved any furniture into that part of the house yet. Besides, she was still trying to stay out of Dan's way down there. She didn't want to give him any more excuses for not getting things finished up. She stared critically at her table situated in her make-shift kitchen. Not very elegant. She wished they could dine in a room with an ocean view. Of course, why not? She leaned the table on its side and rolled it down the hall to the bedroom right beside her own. She set up the table right next to the west window. Perfect! She'd been keeping this room vacant with the plan of restoring it herself into a nice guest room, but for now it would double as her dining room. She set the table carefully, positioning both chairs with access to the lovely view. She even ran downstairs again to clip some pansies and ivy from her planters to create a small bouquet for the centerpiece. Finally she stepped back and admired her handiwork. It wasn't McKenzie's, but it was nice.

She glanced at her watch. It was almost six-thirty. After all her running and moving furniture she felt gritty and grimy. She'd have to hurry to shower and fix up a bit. She really wanted tonight to be special.

She quickly towel dried her hair, allowing it to fall over her shoulders and down her back in damp ringlets. There was no time to dry it completely, or even to style it. Fortunately, it was still very warm and balmy, and her natural curls had a way of curling around her face. She opened her window to let in some fresh air. No cool evening breeze had picked up from the sea yet. It was unusual for the Oregon coast, but nice. It would be a perfect evening for a walk on the beach.

She searched through her closet, not sure what she was looking for. She thought she wanted something soft and feminine, and yes, romantic. Finally, she slipped on a silk sun dress with embroidery on the bodice and tiny pearl buttons down the back. It was a very pale shade of peach, and reminded her of the inside of a seashell. The fabric felt wonderful, as smooth as cream. She looked into the mirror and gave a little twirl, sending the long hem of the skirt swirling around. Just right. She studied her face void of makeup. Jack had always said that a well-dressed woman never went out without full makeup. But lately, she had worn less and less. Mostly she just applied a little mascara, lip gloss, and sometimes a bit of blush. She smoothed on some moisturizer and looked again at her reflection.

Suddenly and unexpectedly she was filled with panic. What could she have been thinking? This was the same dress that Jack had said made her look like a frumpy peasant girl. And just look at her hair, hanging all over the place like an unruly mop.

"Hello," called Quin's deep voice from below. "I knocked, but no one answered and I let myself in. Are you there, Kestra?"

She looked at her clock. He was early! She stuck her head out the door and called out, "I'm up here, but I'm not ready. Can you make yourself at home down there?"

"No problem, I came early. Take your time."

She ran back to her closet and ransacked through her clothes until she found a sophisticated designer dress in a strong shade of turquoise. It had never been a favorite, but she knew it was a good cut and looked nice on her. She struggled to pull on hosiery and matching shoes, then quickly twisted her still damp hair into a tight french roll. She applied makeup and jewelry and looked in the mirror again. This would be the exact routine she had used when going out with Jack, but the image that looked back from the mirror caught her completely off-guard.

Everything was all wrong. Totally wrong! But there was no time to change again. What was wrong with her anyway? After all, this was a perfectly respectable dress. And it hadn't come cheap! And why was she so consumed with her appearance?

She hurried on over to the kitchen, despising the sound of her heels clicking across the hardwood floor. She quickly prepared the salmon for broiling. "Come on up, if you like, Quin," she called as she squeezed lemon juice onto the fillets. "I'm just putting the fish on to broil." She looked around the kitchen for an apron, but there was none to be found. Probably in a box somewhere.

"I'll be up in a couple minutes," he called back.

She sighed in relief as she started to slice a loaf of baguette french bread that she had picked up at the bakery that morning. Maybe she could still get everything under control before Quin came upstairs. She stopped in midslice and laid down the knife. What was she thinking? She needed to get the asparagus water ready to boil! She ran back to her bathroom and filled the saucepan with water, then dashed back and put it on the hot plate. The broiler was hot now. She slid in the fish onto the rack, then moaned. Why hadn't she planned this all out better? Jack had lectured her many times about the importance of staging her dishes so that everything would get done at once. She had wanted tonight to be perfect, and now everything seemed to be going wrong.

She noticed the basket of fresh unwashed strawberries still sitting on the buffet. She wanted to use them for dessert. Once again, she dashed back to her bathroom. Halfway there she realized that she could take the coffeepot to fill now for after dinner. Oh, what she would do for a real kitchen! In what she hoped was her last sprint from bathroom to kitchen, she almost ran into Quin. Water from the coffeepot sloshed out and splattered onto the floor. Quin stood in the hallway with a puzzled expression.

"Need any help?" he asked. Kestra stood in the doorway, coffeepot in one hand, colander of dripping strawberries in the other. She quickly inventoried his casual-looking cords and chambray shirt with sleeves rolled up. He looked comfortable.

"Was this supposed to be a formal dinner?" He looked at her dress then held out his hands apologetically. She wanted to laugh. She wanted to cry. Instead she shook her head speechlessly.

"Do I smell smoke?" he asked, turning toward the makeshift kitchen. Sure enough, smoke poured from the small broiler oven.

"The fish!" She shrieked, running past him. She jerked open the oven door to allow even bigger billows of smoke to escape as she pulled out the smoldering fillets. They were black and crusty on top. And the smell was atrocious! Just then the pan on the burner bubbled over and splashed hot water on top of the buffet. At this point, she turned to Quin and opened her mouth to apologize but instead burst into tears.

"It's okay," he spoke soothingly as he held her and patted her back. "It's really no big deal. I like blackened catfish, so maybe I'll like blackened salmon, too."

She pulled back and looked at him. She knew she probably had mascara running down her cheeks, but she just didn't care anymore. "I wanted everything to—to be perfect," she sobbed.

"Why?"

"I—I don't know why." She tried to stop crying, but it just kept coming, as if some dam had broken loose and wouldn't quit flowing. He held her again, and after what felt like a long time, her tears finally stopped. He handed her a handkerchief, and she blew her nose. The evening was ruined.

"Kestra, do you think I want everything to be perfect?"

She shrugged and dabbed at her eyes. "Don't you?"

He laughed. "What is perfect anyway?"

She shook her head.

"Come here." He led her to the stairs and gently set her down on the top step, sitting down beside her. "First of all, tell me why you are dressed like this? You don't usually dress like this. You look like you're going to some ladies' tea, or fund-raising dinner, or the Emmy awards, or something." He laughed, and to her surprise, she did, too.

"It's so silly. I'm sure you don't really want to hear about it."

"Try me."

And so she did. She told him the whole story of getting dressed the first time, and then thinking about what Jack would have said, and how it made her change everything.

"But as soon as I saw myself in the mirror for the second time, I knew it was all wrong, but it was too late."

"Is it too late now?"

"You mean to change?"

"Would that make you more comfortable?"

She nodded. "Do you mind?"

"Of course not."

"What about dinner? I think I ruined the fish."

"Why don't you go put on something that makes you feel better, and I'll go see if there's any hope for the fish. If not, maybe we can give it an honorable burial at sea."

She dashed back to the bedroom and quickly washed her face, pulled on the silk sun dress, and let her hair fall loosely down her back. It felt so much better. She didn't even put on shoes!

"I'm back!" she announced. He looked at her and broke into a slow smile.

"You look absolutely beautiful," he said quietly. "How do you feel now?"

"I feel like me again."

"That's good. Now, I think the fish is still edible. And your water is still hot, but I don't know what you wanted to put in it."

"I have some asparagus—" She stopped when she saw his face. "You don't like asparagus?"

He made a crooked grin with a wrinkled nose. "Not much. But you go ahead and make it for you."

She laughed. "The truth is, I don't like it much either. I was probably making it for Jack."

Together they took the food to the table. He complimented her on the view and the salad, and they ate well-done salmon and bread and butter. Finally she brought in ice-cream and strawberries for dessert, along with freshly ground French roast coffee.

"Not a very fancy dessert," she apologized.

"Fancy enough for me, I just happen to love fresh strawberries and vanilla ice-cream!"

"Me, too."

"Now, tell me, Kestra, why is it that Jack still has such a hold on you?"

191

"Does he?"

"It sure seems like it. He pops into your conversation on a regular basis. And just look at tonight."

"I suppose you're right." She looked down at the china cup in her hand, tracing her finger over the small gold "M" that stood for "McKenzies." Another thing that Jack had picked out.

"Are you still in love with Jack?"

The serious tone of his voice caught her by surprise, and she looked up to find him gazing steadily into her eyes. She felt herself catch her breath. Not because of the question, but because of the intensity of his stare.

"No," she answered evenly, letting out her breath and setting down her cup.

"Then why do you still let him rule your life?"

"I don't know. Guilt maybe." It surprised her to say this. But as soon as the word was out, she knew it was true.

He nodded slowly without speaking. She wasn't sure if he really understood. She wasn't even sure if she understood.

"Do you want to talk about it, Kestra? I don't want to push you. But if it would help, I'm here."

"It seems like you know everything else about me. You might as well hear this. To tell you the truth, I think it's just hitting me right now."

"Sometimes it helps to say things out loud. It makes you understand your feelings better. But if you'd rather not, I'd certainly understand…"

"No, I want to talk about it." Kestra looked at the candle sputtering as the flame licked at the wax. In many ways her memories of Jack seemed like another lifetime, but in other ways it was almost as if she could feel his breath against her ear.

She spoke slowly, deliberately, almost as if she were navigating her way through a maze. "Jack was a good man. He loved me.

And he wanted to take care of me. But he expected certain things from me. And often it felt like he wanted to change me, to make me into something or someone else." She looked into Quin's eyes. "You see he was quite a perfectionist. And he was much older than I. He had money and power. And I was so thankful and grateful to have someone like him to love me. And take care of me..." She paused, grasping for the words.

"But..." he continued, and his eyes were full of compassion.

"But I was never sure that I loved him—really loved him. I told myself that I did before we were married, but afterwards I questioned whether I really loved Jack, or if it was just the idea of Jack. It was so reassuring to have a wealthy powerful man who loved me and wanted me."

"And is that where the guilt came in?"

"Exactly. And because I felt guilty about not really loving him, or maybe not loving him enough, I was willing to try to remake myself into whatever he wanted me to be. I figured it was the least I could do. Sort of a payoff."

"So were you ever happy with him?"

"Happy?" She looked out over the sea. "I guess I wouldn't have used that word exactly. I mean we had some good times. He took me all over. He exposed me to art, music, fine food, culture, whatever. But I always felt sort of, I don't know how to describe it exactly. Artificial?"

Quin nodded slowly. "That must have been hard."

"It was."

"How did you feel when you knew Jack was dying?"

"Horrible. I was torn apart with guilt for not having really loved him, then torn again for feeling slightly relieved that it would soon all be over, then I was torn all over again because I knew I would miss him. And yet even then, I knew I'd miss him more for what he did than for who he was. Isn't that awful? You must think I'm a horrible person." Her eyes dropped down. She had just unloaded her darkest ugliest secret. Perhaps now Quin would walk away and never speak to her again.

"Do you really think Jack loved you?" said Quin.

She looked up. What could he mean? Of course Jack loved her. Hadn't she just told Quin so? "I don't understand what you mean."

"Well, how can you be so certain that Jack loved you, if he was so eager to change you? Is it possible that he only loved the perfect Kestra that he was trying to create? Did he even know the real Kestra?"

"I don't know if I even know the real Kestra."

"When you really love someone, don't you love them just as they are?"

"But what if they have faults?"

"When you love someone, do you focus on their faults?"

She thought about the way she felt about him. Just that day, Holly had strongly hinted that Kestra wasn't seeing him for who he really was. "So do you mean to say that love is blind, or only sees through rose-colored glasses?"

"No, not exactly. But I think true love will try to see the best in a person. Sure they want to see that person grow and expand, but most of all they just want to be with them, to enjoy them for who they are without trying to change everything about them."

"I think I know what you mean. But maybe there are levels of love. Maybe Jack loved me but at a different level."

"If that's true, maybe you loved him, too, but at a different level."

"Do you really think so?" She felt a spark of hope.

"Why not?"

"I'd like to think I loved Jack. I always tell myself that I loved him. But I still hope that there's another kind of love—

something bigger and deeper than what Jack and I had. Otherwise, I'd probably never want to marry again." Her cheeks grew warm. Their conversation had taken some unpredictable turns and was winding up on shaky ground.

"So do you think there is something bigger and deeper?"

She looked down again. This was uncomfortable. "Yes," she spoke softly, almost afraid to say the word.

"So do I." He stood up and reached for her hand. "Thank you for a very nice dinner, Kestra." She stood and looked up into his eyes, not wanting this moment to end.

"Now it's time for me to show you your surprise."

"The surprise! I almost forgot all about it."

He led her downstairs to the library, and there above the fireplace stood the mantle, beautifully restored.

"Oh, Quin, it's beautiful."

"You can still see some of the smoke damage." He traced his finger over a dark section in the middle. "But I sort of like it. I think it adds character."

"I think so, too. In fact, it makes it even more valuable to me. I can imagine the people in the past who may have built fires right here in this room. Just think, that smoke damage could be a hundred years old. It reminds me that this house has a history."

"I thought we might like to test it out." Quin bent over to a neatly arranged pile of wood on top of crumpled newspaper and lit a match. "I know you don't need a fire tonight, but I thought you might enjoy it."

"Thanks."

They stood together watching the flames dance. The rich wood grain of the mantle seemed to glow in the firelight. Kestra imagined how it would feel to curl up with a good book by this fireplace next winter. She looked over at Quin, his profile illuminated by the gold flickering light. She hoped that he would be part of that cozy picture. He seemed to fit so perfectly with this house, with her.

⤳ 24 ⤲

Kestra awoke early the next morning. She pulled on her sweats and took Riley down to the beach. She replayed last night as she ran. It had started out like such a fiasco, but then it had ended so wonderfully with a moonlit walk on the beach. This same beach! She replayed the moment when she and Quin had almost reached the jetty. They had both stopped walking and turned to look at one another. She would always remember the dark shadows of his face in the moonlight. She had even tilted her chin slightly, as if inviting a kiss. But just then Riley had bounded up and thrown both paws on her legs with a big wet stick in his mouth. Quin had taken the stick and thrown it. And they had both walked back in silence.

"I'm going to have to train you, Riley," she called to him as they raced back up the beach toward the steps. He looked up with loyal brown eyes, his tongue lolling out one side as he romped along.

She had half expected a second chance back at the house. But Quin had simply taken her hand in his and thanked her for a lovely evening. And she had to admit, it had been a lovely evening.

She and Riley started up the beach steps. The sun was just beginning to emerge from the light blanket of fog. It promised to be another beautiful day. She glanced at her watch. There was still time to make it to church. Should she invite Quin to join her? She sprinted up the last steps two at a time, and at the top she practically tumbled into Quin's arms.

"Whoa!" he called, catching her as she fell forward.

"Oh, I'm sorry," she said breathlessly. "I didn't even see you!" She lingered in his arms for just a split second, then stepped back with reluctance.

"What's the hurry?"

"I was just thinking about making it to church this morning." She looked up at him and knew this was her chance. "Would you want to come with me? It's really a nice church. And I think you'd like it."

He cleared his throat. "Actually, I was just looking for you. Remember yesterday, when I said I'd pick up a paper and check the ads for horses. Well, I just called a ranch over in Diggs that's going out of business—bankruptcy sale." He laughed and shook his head. "Remember what I told you about horses being expensive? Anyway, I made an appointment for eleven. And it sounds like the horses will be going fast at these prices. I thought you might want to come along. Maybe we could pick up some breakfast along the way."

"I'd love to. Are you sure it's not too much trouble?"

"No trouble. Like I said, I wouldn't mind having a horse myself."

She smiled. "And I suppose that doesn't have anything to do with Page's dream of having horses here."

"Page is a good girl. But she still needs some things in her life to help keep her out of trouble. Her job is good for her, and I know she's starting to go to youth group. But it's okay to have a passion for something that's just plain fun, too."

"I couldn't agree with you more!"

"Then why don't you go get ready. I have to go make a couple of phone calls."

She wanted to ask him who he needed to call on a Sunday morning but knew it wasn't any of her business. Instead, she walked back to the house. Halfway there she saw Dan's pickup. She was sure he hadn't come to work today. What could he possibly want? Hopefully nothing was wrong with the house renovation.

"Hi ya, Kestra," he called in a friendlier than usual voice.

"Hi, Dan. What'cha up to?"

"I was just dropping by to see if you wanted to come to church with me. We haven't seen you there for a while, and Matthew wondered if everything was going okay with you."

She glanced at her watch. "It's early for church."

"Yeah, I know. I thought I'd look around and see if we're ready for the tile man to come and lay the tile for the kitchen. I saw him yesterday, and he said he has the first part of the week available if we're ready."

"Really?" She stepped up with fresh interest. It would be great to see the tile get laid. She could just imagine the clean black and white checkerboard tiles in the big kitchen.

"Yep. Care if I come in and check it out?"

"Of course, come on in!" She opened the door and let him in. "You go ahead and do whatever you need to do. I'm going to take a shower. I've been running, and I'm a mess." She dashed upstairs.

This was great news! Dan was getting back into the swing of things with her house. Maybe he was actually changing.

After a long hot shower, Kestra wrapped a big white towel around herself and walked into her bedroom. Riley stood before her half-opened bedroom door with his feet spread apart in a defensive stance. His white teeth showed as he growled at

199

something she couldn't see. She knew she hadn't left the door open.

"Who's there?" she asked. "Dan, is that you?" She heard footsteps in the hall, but she couldn't tell if they were coming or going. "Dan, is that you?" she called again.

The door moved slightly, and Kestra clutched the towel tighter and drew back into the bathroom. "Kestra, is everything okay?" called Dan's voice.

"Yes, fine," she answered firmly. "Riley was just acting strange. Close the door, please. I'm just getting out of the shower." She listened, but did not hear the door close. "Dan?"

"Yeah?"

"I said, CLOSE the door!" The door slammed shut. Kestra shook her head. Maybe she was overreacting, but just the same, the whole thing was unsettling. She pulled on jeans and a sweater and ran downstairs to give him a piece of her mind.

"What are you doing prowling around my house, Dan Hackett?" she demanded when she finally found him standing in the library studying the refinished mantle.

"Prowling? I just came up to ask you something."

"What?"

"I still wondered if you wanted to go to church with me." He looked at her with clear blue eyes and a choirboy expression.

She shook her head slowly. "Sorry, I can't go with you. I have other plans."

"What kind of plans?"

She could never get used to the fact that Dan had absolutely no inhibition about asking blunt nosy questions and expecting civilized answers. Maybe the best way to deal with him was to give a straight answer and then hopefully move on.

"I'm going to look at some horses this morning," she announced.

"Horses?" he said the word as if they were talking about space aliens from Pluto.

"You know, those four-legged critters that cowboys ride. They have a tail and mane."

"Why are you looking at horses?" He asked in a suspicious tone. What difference could it possibly make to him why she wanted to look at horses?

"I'm looking at horses with an interest in buying one or two. You know I have the stable, and—"

"Just because you have a stable, you think you need to get horses? Kestra, are you nuts? You don't even have this house done and you're going out to buy horses? Tell me one good reason you need to get horses."

She wondered why she felt the need to tell him anything. But like a child called before the principal she went on. "For one thing, Page knows a lot about horses, and she would really like to have one to take care of—"

"You don't mean to tell me, you are going out to buy horses just because that little beatnik with the pierced nose wants one. Kestra, I think you need serious help."

That was the last straw! "Dan Hackett, it's none of your stinking business! And you are totally out of line to talk to me like this!" She prepared herself for a whopper of a fight now. She had asked for it, and she was ready to take him on. But instead, he just stood silently, staring blankly at the mantle piece.

"I'm sorry, Kestra. You're absolutely right."

Her eyes popped open and she felt her jaw drop. Dan Hackett saying he was sorry and that she was right? Stepping down from a good fight? This was too much!

He looked back at her. "I guess I just care about you, Kestra. I don't want to see you do something you'll regret."

She tried to regain her composure and speak. "Apology

accepted. Sorry if I overreacted."

He smiled. "That's okay. I should know better than to push your buttons like that. You know, since I started going to church and Bible study, I'm starting to see life differently."

She wanted to ask him if he had totally surrendered his life to Jesus and become a Christian, but she couldn't make herself form the words. For one thing, she hated being nosy. But perhaps even more, she didn't really want to know. The fact that Dan Hackett was an unbeliever had always made a very comfortable excuse for not getting involved again. That, and the fact that he drove her crazy so much of the time. But what if he had changed?

"Who did this?" he asked, pointing to the mantle.

"Quin refinished it. Didn't he do a nice job?"

"I suppose, but what a waste of time." He traced the darkened wood where years of smoke had left its mark. "See, I told you, you could never get that to come out."

"I didn't want it to come out. I like it just the way it is. I think it has character. Everything doesn't have to be perfect and new, you know. I happen to like antiques and old things that have a story behind them. This house for instance. I never want it to be all perfect. I want to see its charm and personality."

He frowned and shook his head. "Good thing, because it would take a fortune to make it perfect. So, what's going on with this Quin guy? Just who is he anyway? And why is he here? I heard Margie Ganz in the coffee shop saying that she saw someone who looked like him on 'America's Most Wanted.'"

She laughed. "Now that is really ridiculous!"

"What makes you so sure? Do you know anything about him? Do you even know what he does for a living?"

"No, but—"

"Well, I say he seems pretty suspicious. He keeps to himself all day, and he doesn't seem to have any kind of job. Yet he seems to have money. That Land Rover must have cost a bundle. Who knows, he might be smuggling drugs. They say there's a lot of cocaine traffic going up and down the Oregon coast right now. And I heard Margie saying that every time he comes to town, he's mailing off some package. Pretty suspicious. You better watch your step, Kestra."

"Thanks for the advice." She knew her voice was hard and cold, but she didn't care. She just wanted him to leave. And she didn't want to lose her temper again.

"So, you need any company to check out these horses? I know a thing or two about—"

"No, thanks."

"You sure? You know how those horse traders might try to take advantage of a sweet little lady like you." The choirboy smile was back.

"I thought you were going to church, Dan."

"I can change my mind."

"Well, thanks anyway. Quin already offered to take me."

His face grew dark, and he turned on his heel and headed for the door. "Well, you better be careful, Kestra. Sometimes people aren't what they seem!"

She listened to his pickup tear out of the driveway. She felt like she wanted to throw something or punch someone.

"Help me to be more patient, Lord," she prayed. Then she remembered how people said praying for patience invites testing. "Can I change that request, Lord? How about if you just help me to be more loving and kind?"

"Hello," called Quin from the front porch through the still-open door. "Are you ready, Kestra?"

"Coming."

She climbed into the Land Rover. It was very nice, with a wood console, cushy leather seats, and CD player. She remembered what Dan had said about drug dealing and chuckled to herself.

"What's the joke?" asked Quin as he started the ignition.

"Oh, it's just silly." She looked over at him. He had slipped on some wire-rimmed sunglasses, and for some reason the glasses together with his dark beard did take on an almost sinister appearance. But she refused to fall for Dan's tricks. Instead she laughed even louder.

"Oh, it was just my old friend, Dan Hackett." She said sarcastically, then turned a little more serious. "He was just here, and he had the nerve to suggest that you might be some sort of felon or drug dealer." She expected him to laugh, or at least smile. He did neither.

"The truth is, Kestra," he spoke without looking at her. "You really don't know very much about me, do you?"

~ 25 ~

Kestra and Quin drove down the highway in an awkward silence. She forced her mind not to replay every negative idea that Dan or even Holly had suggested about Quin's character or lack of it. She knew him better than that. And she wasn't the least bit worried. Or was she?

"It is true," he continued. "You don't know much about me. Not really."

"I know what I need to know."

"And what is that?"

"That you are good and kind, and I can trust you."

The tiny lines around his eyes crinkled as the corners of his mouth tipped up, and she sighed in relief. They drove along in silence again. But this time it was a comfortable silence. Kestra knew the words she said were true. She did trust him. It did bother her that she didn't know much about him. But where could she begin?

"So why don't you just ask me?" said Quin.

She turned in surprise. "Did you use to work in the circus as a fortune teller?"

He chuckled. "Sorry. It wasn't that difficult, it was written all over your face."

"What?"

"Your curiosity." He turned and glanced at her. "Dan may have stirred you up a little, but you have to admit, it's been there all along. What surprises me is that you never ask."

She folded and unfolded her hands in her lap. She knew he was right, but she wasn't exactly sure why she hadn't felt comfortable enough to ask. "I guess I never felt like you wanted me to ask. You know how sometimes there's an open door and someone's waving for you to come on in." She turned and looked at him.

He nodded knowingly. "I guess, I haven't really had an open door, have I?"

"It didn't feel like it."

"I'm sorry."

"It's okay. Actually, I think I was comfortable not knowing too much about you."

"Why?"

"I don't know. Maybe it feels safer that way."

"Like a protective hedge that keeps you from getting too involved?"

"Exactly."

He pulled into the restaurant and they walked inside. Suddenly, it felt like they were entering a new place in their relationship, and Kestra wasn't quite sure she wanted to go there. She had been enjoying things the way they were. She realized that she liked the mystery attached to Quin. It made her a little freer to be who she wanted to be or maybe to discover who she was.

She made small talk as they ate, telling him about the tile man who might be coming the next day, and how she hoped that Dan was back on track as far as the renovation went. She even told him about how Dan had actually apologized to her today.

"Maybe he's turning over a new leaf," said Quin as they walked back to the Land Rover.

Kestra continued to chat about everything and anything she could think of, but she carefully navigated around any questions that might reveal too much information about Quin. She just wasn't ready for that. Before long, they were driving under a sign that said 'Leaning J Ranch.'

They both perched on the pole fence of the corral and watched as an older man named Hank showed them his horses. He wore dusty jeans and sharp-toed boots, and his belt buckle looked big enough to serve dinner on. Hank explained that these were quarterhorses—a cowboy's working horse—fast, dependable, and very maneuverable. Several had even been trained for barrel racing, but those would cost more. Kestra was certain that she had never seen anything so beautiful as the dozen horses that galloped across the corral, their hooves thundering on the hard-packed earth, the soft green hills like a backdrop behind them. She felt sorry for Hank, she could see the pain in his eyes as he talked about getting out of the business.

"I really don't know much about horses," admitted Kestra as Hank leaned against the fence, tipping his hat low to shade his eyes. She looked out on the horses as they settled down and nosed around the fence posts for grass. "I think I'd like a couple of horses to use for trail rides for guests that will come to my restaurant."

Hank frowned. "What kind of trails you talkin' about?"

"Well, there's a slightly steep trail that leads down to the beach. And then there's a nice long strip of beach."

He rubbed his chin. "A beach?"

"Yes, I thought people could take the horses down and ride them on the beach."

"Well now, that wouldn't be too bad. You see, these horses need to stretch out their legs once in a while. A beach ride might be right nice for that." He looked out on the horses with what seemed to be a mixture of love and pride. "I'd just hate to see them get stuck in a stable day-in-day-out with no place to run. You say you only got two fenced-in acres. That ain't much room for runnin'. But if they could go down to the beach…"

Kestra glanced at Quin. "How exactly do you do this," she asked quietly, "this horse dickering business?"

Quin lifted his brows. "Are you thinking you're interested in one of them?"

She pointed to a reddish brown horse with a dark mane. "I like that one over there. Is that a chestnut?"

"You mean that pretty sorrel mare?" asked Hank, his eyes sparking with interest. "That's Annie. She's a real sweet horse. Not a mean bone in her body. She's eight years old. She's not the fastest thing on four legs, but she's trustworthy. Want to see her up close?"

Kestra climbed over the fence and followed Hank over to Annie. The horse came right up to them and nuzzled her nose in Hank's hand. Kestra stroked the smooth side of Annie's cheek.

"Hi, Annie," said Kestra. "You're a real pretty girl." Annie turned her head gracefully and seemed to look right at Kestra with large chocolate eyes rimmed in long lashes. Kestra ran her hand down Annie's dark mane then turned to Hank. "How much for Annie?"

Before they drove away from the Leaning J, Kestra had become the proud owner of three horses and several second-hand saddles and tack. First, she couldn't leave without Annie's best friend, Chip, a handsome bay gelding. Then she noticed a horse that seemed to stay close to Annie, almost as if they were friends. Hank explained that particular horse was getting old and probably no one would buy her. But he said she'd been a good horse in her time and still had "plenty of ridin' left in her." He named a price that Kestra couldn't refuse. Kestra had gone back to tell Annie good-bye for now. She couldn't wait to get better acquainted with her.

"Hank said he could deliver all four by the end of next week," announced Quin as he pulled onto the main road.

"All *four?*"

"Yes, I hope you don't mind that I'm getting one, too."

"Really? I didn't even notice you looking. Which one? No, don't tell me, let me guess." She closed her eyes and tried to remember the other horses. "Aha! I know which one!"

"Really? Which one do you think it is?"

"If I remember right, it seems his name was Othello!"

Quin threw back his head and laughed. "I guess you know more about me than I thought. Of course, you would know that I'd go with the dark horse!"

"Really? Are you a dark horse? Is that how you see yourself?"

His brow creased as he shook his head. "No, the truth is, I just happen to think that Othello is one beautiful horse."

"I have to agree with you there. But he was a little too big and strong looking for my taste. He was almost scary. It seemed like too much force to be contained in one animal."

"Maybe. But he seemed well trained. And there's nothing wrong with a good strong horse that knows how to behave. By the way, have you ever actually been on a horse?"

She grinned. "What do you think?"

"My guess would be 'not,' but then again, I think you might have a few surprises up your sleeve."

"Actually, I took riding lessons in Seattle before Jack died.

He felt it was important for me to be comfortable on a horse. I don't know much about riding western style. I only rode English."

"Switching from English to western is a piece of cake. In fact, English may be the best way to learn how to get a feel for the horse since English saddles are so much lighter, plus you establish a better sense of balance. But I'll give you some tips for western. I've ridden both English and western, but western seems to be more popular on the West Coast. The most important thing is that you feel comfortable on a horse."

"I guess I'm fairly comfortable. Actually, Annie seems so sweet, I'll probably be very comfortable with her. Just don't ever expect me to saddle up that Othello!"

Quin laughed. "Yes, you better steer clear of those dark horses."

∽ 26 ∼

The next morning, Dan and the crew were hard at work even before the sun was up. Kestra didn't know whether to sneak down and take a peak at their progress, or just stay out of their way. Finally she decided to make fudge. It was the only thing she could think of that could be made in the microwave that the workers might like.

It seemed pretty quiet downstairs by the time she came down. She hoped they hadn't all given up and gone home. As she approached the dining room, she noticed that the large appliances were no longer stacked along the walls. She poked her head around the doorway to the kitchen and couldn't believe her eyes. The appliances were all in place, and the tile man was already at work. It was amazing. It actually looked like a kitchen now.

"Hey, there," called the man from his knees. "You won't want to walk on this floor right now. I've got it all prepped for laying this tile."

"I see." She stepped into the doorway, careful not to let her foot touch the kitchen area. "This looks great!"

"Well, it's a little early to get the full effect, but I think it will be nice."

She gazed dreamily at the black and white checkerboard tiles and the sleek appliances set into the dark cherry wood cabinets. It was a nice mix of old and new. With the copper ceiling above, it promised to be a beautiful kitchen.

"Is Dan still around?"

"Nah, he and the guys had to go put a roof on somewhere in town. But that's okay. It's better not to have folks around when I'm setting tile."

She wondered if that meant her, too. She set the fudge on an upside-down crate. "I made this for you guys. Help yourself, if you like." She turned and went outside to find Riley. She was glad she had let him out straight away. The tile man might not be too happy if Riley came flying through and messed up his work. She whistled for Riley, but he didn't come. She walked over to the beach steps and looked down. Surely, he wouldn't go down there without her. She glanced over at the cottage. She knew that Riley loved Quin and knew where he lived. Perhaps...

She knocked on the door, careful not to look through the window from the porch. She really didn't want to invade his privacy.

He opened the door with an odd look on his face. His hair was ruffled, almost like it hadn't been combed since he got up, but it didn't look bad. He had on a wrinkled denim shirt with shirttails hanging over well-worn cords. It didn't look as if he had been sleeping, but he had sort of a dazed expression. And he said nothing. Just looked at her blankly, almost as if he didn't know her. It was rather unnerving.

"I'm sorry to disturb you," she spoke quickly, feeling very much the intruder. "I couldn't find Riley, and I thought maybe... Of course, he's not here. I'm sorry."

Quin blinked his eyes and scratched his head. "Haven't seen him. Let me know if he doesn't show up."

"Yes, I will. Thanks. Sorry again to bother you."

"It's okay."

She turned and walked away, listening for the door to close. As it did so, she tried to shake off the odd feeling the encounter had given her. She walked around the grounds to the stable, whistling and calling for Riley. Where could he be? Suddenly, she grew very worried. What if something had happened to him? What if he had climbed on the rock wall by the path and fallen over the cliff. Her heart pounded with fear as she raced over to the wall. She leaned and looked down and saw only the surf pounding against the rocks as it always did. But it was still possible that he could have fallen and tried to swim to safety.

She raced to the beach steps and ran down recklessly, imagining Riley drowning in the pounding surf. She ran north to where the rocks came around and ended the long strip of beach. She knew that the other side contained the churning surf where the cliff behind her house fell to the sea, but she also knew that it would be dangerous to try to climb over the rocks. Again, she saw Riley in her mind's eye, bleeding and broken. She ran through the knee-deep surf and quickly scaled the rocks. Though slick and wet, they had jagged places in which to place her hands and feet. Before she knew it, she had covered a few yards and was very near the top.

"*Kestra!*" A voice bellowed above the sound of the waves, and she turned to see Quin. Just as she turned, she felt her right foot slip off the rock and the next thing she knew she was falling.

"QUIN!" she screamed. She felt her head hit a rock as she plummeted downward. Everything became a blur. Then nothing.

～ 27 ～

She opened her eyes and looked around. Where was she? The room looked familiar. Oh, yes, it was her bedroom in the caretaker's cottage. But then she remembered she didn't live here anymore. How did she get here? Something cold and damp tickled her hand, and she looked down to see Riley nudging her with his wet nose.

"You're okay," she said with relief. She moved her hand to stroke his head and noticed the deep scrape across her wrist. Suddenly her head throbbed in pain, and it all came back to her.

"Thank God, you're all right," Quin came in and sat down beside her. "I just called the hospital. I tried to call 911 but apparently that doesn't work around here. They're sending an ambulance right away."

She touched her forehead and felt the lump. "I don't need an ambulance. The only thing that hurts is my head."

"Kestra, you took quite a fall. I'm surprised you didn't break bones. And I don't know what came over me because I know better." He looked down at his feet. "I think I was in shock. I just ran over and scooped you up and ran you up here."

"Thank you."

"No, don't thank me. I could have killed you. I know the first rule in an injury like this is to leave the injured person immobile. But you were just lying limp in the water, and I guess you could have drowned, even as shallow as it was…"

"Then you saved my life."

"No, Kestra. It's my fault that you fell in the first place. If I hadn't called out, you probably would have been okay." He took her hand gently in his. "I don't know what came over me. Usually, I think very carefully about everything I do. In this case, it feels like I just lost my head. I'm so sorry."

"It's really okay, Quin. I'm the one to be sorry. I should never have climbed up there. I was just so worried about Riley." She turned and looked at her dog. "I thought maybe he had fallen over the cliff. I imagined him drowning in the surf, not being able to swim past the rocks."

"After you left, I saw Riley wandering around. So I looked for you and thought maybe you'd gone down to the beach to search for him. When I saw you up there, I yelled out your name without thinking that I might startle you like that. I'm so sorry. Are you really okay?"

She sat up. "Yes, I think I'm fine. Just a little sore and a whopper of a headache. But really, I'm okay. Will you please call the hospital and tell them I don't need an ambulance?"

"Okay, I'll call them and see what they think."

He was gone for several minutes. Long enough for her to gaze around the room that she had once slept in. It looked a little different now. Sparser, more masculine. There was a Bible on the dresser. She smiled and leaned her head back on the pillow. Her clothes were soaking. She could see where he had taken off her socks and shoes and tossed them to the floor. Even though she was wrapped in a wool blanket she was still cold.

"I just talked to an ER nurse, and she said she would only

call back the ambulance if I promised to stay with you and check these things." He held up a list that he must have just jotted down. "I told her I was willing. Are you?"

Kestra nodded, shivering.

"First of all, I don't think you should try to go home yet, but you need to get out of those wet things." He opened the door to the tiny closet and rummaged around until he found a plaid flannel shirt. "Wear this for now." He held it up and it looked long enough to go to her knees. "Now you're sure you're okay? Do you need any help? The nurse said it was best for you not to move very much, that you most likely have a slight concussion."

She shook her head, then instantly wished she hadn't. "Do you have any pain reliever?"

"Right, the nurse said to give you some Tylenol. I'll go get it. And she suggested ice packs for your bruises, and then I'll take a look at that cut on your arm."

"Thanks."

"Sure, Nurse Quin at your service." He bowed. "Call if you need any help." This was followed by a cute grin that made her smile despite the pain that throbbed in her head.

She had to climb out of bed to peel off her wet sweats. It was quite an ordeal, and she considered calling Quin to help, but she wasn't ready for that much intimacy. Finally she slipped into the soft flannel shirt. It felt warm and fuzzy against her chilled skin, and it smelled like Quin. She buttoned it up and looked back at the bed. She could see that it had gotten wet from her clothing, and it looked anything but inviting. Just then she felt her head begin to swim, and the room swirled around her.

"Quin!" she cried out as she felt herself falling again.

She never touched the ground this time. Quin burst through the door and caught her just as the room was going black.

She awoke on the couch with a quilt tucked snugly around her. Quin was hunched over the fireplace coaxing flames from a small stack of kindling. Her head was still throbbing, but at least she was getting warmer now. She studied his back as he wadded up another piece of newspaper. He still had on his wrinkled denim shirt, but she could see how broad his shoulders and back were. Too bad she'd been unconscious when he carried her from the beach. It would have been nice to have felt that strength. He turned and looked at her, and she felt her cheeks grow warm. She hoped he wasn't reading her thoughts.

"How are you feeling?" he asked. "I was giving you five more minutes, and then I was going to call the ambulance again."

"I'm sorry. I really am a lot of trouble. You probably should have just left me down on the beach."

He smiled. "Well, at least you're getting your sense of humor back. You must be feeling a little better." He handed her a couple of pills and a cool glass of water. "I've got some tea brewing. My mother was a firm believer that tea was the cure-all for just about anything." He went into the kitchen, and Kestra looked around the living room. It was messier than when she had lived here. Papers and boxes were here and there, a lap-top computer was sitting on the table. She noticed several Patrick O'Riley books splayed across the floor as if they had been looked at recently.

He came back and placed a mug of tea in her hands and pulled up a chair next to the couch. "I took the liberty of adding a little honey."

She took a sip. "Mmm, good. Thanks."

"The nurse said you should stay still and drink plenty of fluids. And I need to observe you."

"Observe me?"

He laughed. "Yes, that should be interesting. Actually, she

said that you'll probably just want to sleep. But I should make sure that you don't sleep too long. She said to wake you up every thirty minutes or so."

"I see." She sipped her tea again. "I noticed you have your Patrick O'Riley books out. Been doing some reading?"

He glanced over his shoulder. "Yes, actually, a little."

"I thought you didn't really like him."

"I never said that."

Again, she was feeling sleepy. She set down her mug. "You said something like that..." She leaned her head back. His face hovered over hers with a look of concern.

"Doing your observing, are you?"

He grinned.

When she awoke again, he had a glass of orange juice waiting for her. "Here you go, drink up."

"Thanks. You make a good nurse." The juice was cool and refreshing. Her head seemed to be throbbing a little less. She sat up and looked at her watch. "Wow, it's almost two. What have you been doing this whole time? Let me guess, you've been reading Patrick O'Riley."

He grinned. "Maybe..."

"So you admit it, you do like him."

"I never said that I didn't."

"Well, you sort of made fun of him."

"Never! For your information, I happen to admire Patrick O'Riley more than almost anyone."

"Really? So do I."

"I think the way he could tell an interesting story to teach about Christ's love was pure genius."

She sighed. "It was reading Patrick O'Riley novels that brought me back to a relationship with Jesus. When I read *The Mark of the Lion* I was so touched. It was like God was speaking to me right through the pages of that book."

218

"Really? It meant that much to you?"

"It helped change my life. It was Patrick O'Riley novels that kept me going through the last months of Jack's illness. In fact, it was *Spring's Awakening* that got me started reading the Bible again. I know the O'Riley books don't contain a lot of heavy theology or anything, but the way he writes feels so on target to me. He makes God seem real."

"Did you know that Patrick O'Riley was also a brilliant theologian in his time?"

"No, but it doesn't surprise me. The most amazing thing is how well his stories relate to today's culture even though they were written a hundred years ago. Either that grandson of his is very talented at revising, or Patrick O'Riley was writing way beyond his time."

"Actually, it's his great-grandson. But I think O'Riley wrote the kind of classic stories that are timeless. They translate across generations and cultures. To tell you the truth, I learned much of my own theology from O'Riley, too."

"Well, then we must agree on a lot." Kestra leaned back and looked across the room to his computer with a stack of papers nearby. "What are you working on?"

"Working on?"

"Yes, what kind of work do you do?" She pointed to the laptop computer on the pine table.

"Oh, just some computer stuff. Not very interesting. Say, I was thinking about going over to your house to get some dry things for you. Do you think you'll be okay if I'm gone a few minutes?"

"Actually, I could probably go back home now." She sat up and leaned forward, but her head began to throb again. She leaned back and Quin placed the coldpack lightly on her forehead.

"Why don't you just take it easy for a while."

"Good idea. Hey, I think Page is working in the carriage

house today. She's helping strip some tables for refinishing. You could ask her to bring me some things. Besides, she's probably wondering where I am."

"I'll see if I can hunt her down."

Kestra leaned back and closed her eyes. Would this horrible headache ever go away? She slipped back to sleep, then was awakened by a loud knocking at the door. Quin didn't seem to be around. Maybe it was Page with her clothes. She slowly got up and walked to the door. She opened it and there stood Dan Hackett with his mouth dropped open as if he'd seen a ghost. She clutched the doorknob with both hands and wondered what he wanted.

"What are you doing here?" he exploded. "And why are you dressed, or should I say *undressed*, like that?"

She stepped back in fear. His voice, so full of anger, made her wonder if he might actually strike her.

"I should have known something like this was going on!" he fumed. "So this is the thanks I get for everything—"

Kestra saw Quin rushing up the porch steps behind Dan. He started to push past him, but Dan blocked his path.

"Excuse me, I need to get in here!" Quin gave Dan a shove and quickly took Kestra by the arm and guided her back to the couch. She sighed in relief. Her head was throbbing, and she felt nauseous. He gently tucked the quilt around her, and just as he was starting to stand, she saw Dan coming at him.

"Quin!" she cried, but it was too late. Dan had lunged with his fist, catching unsuspecting Quin right in the chin. Kestra screamed in horror. But Quin quickly recovered, blocking the next blow with his forearm. Before Dan could strike again, Quin grabbed him by the shirt and shoved him out the door.

"And don't come back without an invitation!" He yelled as he slammed the door. He turned to Kestra and rubbed his chin. "What is that guy's problem? Is there something going on between you two that I should know about?"

"Nothing I haven't already told you about. Are you okay, Quin?"

"Just a bruise. See, beards are good for something."

"I like your beard."

He smiled. "Thanks."

"Sorry about Dan. I don't know how I can make my feelings any clearer to him. It's almost as if he has this obsession. I even wonder about his new interest in church. I hope it's sincere, but I guess I don't quite trust him."

"Under the circumstances, I don't think you should."

Suddenly she recalled yesterday's incident when she was getting out of the shower. What exactly had he been up to? Quin was right, she had better not trust him. If only the house renovation were completed, then she could wash her hands of him once and for all.

Another knock at the door startled her. This time Quin answered, careful to crack the door a little at first, then wider.

"Hello, Page," he said warmly. "Come on in."

She walked in, glancing nervously over her shoulder. "Boy, you should have just seen Dan Hackett. I think someone's having a bad day. He tore out of here like a madman. I hope he doesn't meet anyone coming in the driveway." She handed Kestra the clothes then knelt beside her. "Are you all right? Quin told me about your fall. Gosh, your head looks pretty bad. You going to be okay?"

"Thanks, Page. I'm feeling much better. I think I ought to be able to go home before long—that is if Nurse Quin will release me from his care."

"I would, but I don't really think you should be alone. Hey, maybe Page could spend the night with you. What do you think, Page?"

"Sure, I'd be glad to. If you want me, Kestra."

Kestra smiled. "That'd be great. Will your mom mind?"

"No, she doesn't even have to work tonight."

"Perfect," said Quin. "Now, I'm going to fix you a little something to eat. In the meantime, I think you have some good news to share with Page."

"That's right. I almost forgot. We're getting horses, Page. Four horses."

"Four horses!" Page shrieked. "You're kidding! Four horses, this is so cool! When will they get here?"

"Not until the end of the week."

Page stood up and danced around. "Horses! Now, you have to keep your word about letting me be your stable girl, right?"

"You bet, I can't pull this off without you."

"Four horses! This is so great. Well, I better get back to work. I've gotten two tables stripped already today. And I need to call Mom and let her know I'm staying over." She opened the door, then turned around. "Four horses!"

Quin laughed from the kitchen. "Doesn't that almost make you wish you'd gotten more?" He came out with a small bowl of soup and some saltines. She sipped a little soup and nibbled at the crackers, but she really wasn't very hungry. She leaned her head back and slipped off to sleep again. When she awoke it was with Quin gently nudging her and looking into her face.

"Kestra, are you okay? I think I should take you in to be checked. I'm getting worried about you." His brow was creased and she could tell his concern was very sincere. She sat up and touched her head. It had finally stopped throbbing.

"I think I'm feeling better, Quin." She looked at her watch. "I can't believe I've been here all day. I'm sorry to have taken so much of your time."

"No, that's not the problem. It's just I was getting so worried about you. You slept for almost two hours that time and your face was so white, and you didn't move—" He looked the other way and she saw him take a deep breath. "I was just very worried, Kestra."

"I appreciate your concern, Quin. I think I'm ready to get dressed, and if you could just help me walk back home, I think I can do it now."

She went into his room and slowly pulled on her jeans and slipped her feet into sandals. So far so good. She stepped out and walked toward the door.

"Here, let me help you." He took her gently, firmly wrapping one strong arm around her back and supporting her as they walked slowly down the porch steps and toward her house.

"I hope you don't mind, I decided to leave your shirt on. I promise I'll return it later. Although, I must admit I'm getting a little attached to it."

"Why don't you keep it then," he said with a smile. "I'd like to think of you wearing it."

Those simple words filled her with a warm feeling that almost erased the aches and pains from her fall. Almost. When they finally reached the stairs in the house, her head was swimming again, but before she could say anything, he swooped her up and carried her up the stairs. Under other circumstances, it could have been so romantic. He gently laid her on top of her bed, and she leaned her head against the cool white pillow and relaxed.

"Just rest. I think I'll stick around for a while and make sure you're okay. Then I'll go hunt down Page and let her know you're up here." He moved around the room a bit, then finally stopped and looked out the window. "This is a very nice room."

She sighed. It was a nice room. But it was even nicer with him in it. She closed her eyes and allowed herself to drift, thinking how wonderful it would be to always have him near like this. She thought the words, and later she even wondered if she had said them out loud. *I love you, Quin. I love you with my whole heart.*

⌁ 28 ⌁

Page took Kestra to see the doctor the next morning. After what seemed like a lengthy exam, he proclaimed her well enough to go home and take it easy for the next couple of days. It was nice having Page around to help out. She made sure Kestra didn't overdo it. It was strange being mothered by a teen, but Kestra didn't mind, and it was good to see Page feeling important and useful. Kestra made it very clear to her that she was needed, and Page seemed to thrive on it.

Holly came over in the middle of the week to check on Kestra's recovery, as well as to admire the progress on the kitchen.

"Kestra, it's absolutely fabulous!" said Holly, running her hand over the white marble countertops. "Very elegant, but also practical. Doesn't it just make you want to cook something marvelous?"

Kestra grinned. "Actually, it does. And I think I'm feeling well enough to give it a try. How about that dinner we talked about with you and Matthew. It could be Matthew's chance to meet Quin."

"I don't want you to go to all that trouble. You're barely getting over your fall and your concussion."

"I'm fine. And besides I can get Page to help. How about Saturday night?"

"Sounds great! What can I bring?"

"Nothing. I will have everything under control."

"Just like that story you told me about fixing dinner for Quin?" teased Holly.

Kestra frowned. "Thanks for reminding me of that. I'll have to remember to share all my humiliations with you. But the question is, are you just coming for my great food or to enjoy our wonderful company?"

"Both."

"Hmm, well I better start planning then."

"When do your horses get here?"

"Oh, that's right. I almost forgot, although I don't know how I could with Page literally counting the days, hours, and minutes." She laughed. "They'll be here Friday morning. Hey, maybe we could all take a ride on Saturday. Maybe you could come a little earlier, maybe bring a change of clothes. Do you know if Matthew likes to ride?"

"Yes, actually, I think he might be pretty good. His mom told me he always wanted to be a cowboy."

"His mom? This is sounding serious, Holly. Any new developments that I should know about?"

Holly glanced around the unfinished dining room. "Well, I think there's still plenty of time to get this room done before the big event. Just keep Dan on track."

Kestra moaned. "Ugh, after what happened on Monday, I wonder how long it will be until Dan comes back to work. I guess I should be thankful that the kitchen got done before his little blow out. It will probably be weeks now before he comes back."

Holly sighed. "Poor Dan. I wonder if he'll come to Bible study now. Matthew was having such great hopes for him. Of course, you never know, this may be just what Dan needs to make him really see his need for the Lord. Broken hearts can work wonders, you know."

"For Dan's sake, I really hope so. I've been praying for him. But I have to keep checking myself to make sure my prayers aren't self-motivated, because I'd really like him to get this house finished and then move on with his life. And out of mine."

"Yeah, what a mess this has turned out to be."

Kestra looked around her unfinished house and sighed. "Sometimes I wonder if I really need to have everything fixed the way Dan originally planned out. These wood floors in the dining room, for instance. Dan says they need to be replaced, but I actually like them. I wonder if we couldn't just refinish them and let them be."

Holly bent down and examined the wood. "Well, it's pretty worn and warped in places, but I've been in restaurants that are worse. I don't know why you couldn't just have them refinished. One thing is for sure, you won't find wood like this anywhere else."

"Maybe I should come up with an alternate plan, just in case Dan tries to make himself scarce again."

"Might not be a bad idea. I have to get back to the shop. I'll see you on Saturday then. Call if you want me to bring anything."

Kestra went out to the carriage house to find Page. She spotted her around the corner, gently rubbing a tabletop with a piece of steel wool. Page was wearing her ever-present overalls, humming as she worked.

"Hi, Page. That looks great."

"Thanks. I thought this one was ready for oil, but now I wonder if it needs one more coat of sealer."

Kestra ran her hand over the top. "It feels fine, Page. Just go ahead with the oil. I think you're turning into a real perfectionist. But keep in mind we have about three dozen of these tables to refinish."

Page groaned, then grinned. "Only two days until the horses come."

Kestra laughed and started sanding another table nearby. "Hey, I'm planning a dinner Saturday night. Do you think you'd want to stay late and help out, maybe spend the night?"

"Sure, that would be fine."

"Page, please don't ever let me take advantage of you. If I ask you to work sometime and you have other plans, I'll understand. I mean, I know you're sixteen. You need to have a life."

Page looked back down at the table she was oiling. "Well, it's not like I have a whole lot of friends right now." She turned to Kestra. "Not that I really care that much. And I think of you as a friend. Even though you're older and stuff."

Kestra smiled. "I think of you as a friend, too, Page. Almost like a younger sister."

"Really?"

Kestra nodded.

"Cool!"

They worked together into the afternoon. Kestra told Page about her plans to get the kitchen set up tomorrow. She explained where things were stored and how she wanted things to be arranged in the kitchen. She planned to start using the kitchen as soon as possible, and certainly by Saturday.

"Hello, ladies!" called Quin from the cottage. "How about taking a break? I've got some iced-tea over here."

"Sounds good," called Kestra.

They sat on his porch and sipped iced-tea as they watched Riley chase a stick each time Quin tossed it. Page talked about how wonderful it would be to have the horses, and Kestra just leaned back and relaxed. There was a fresh breeze blowing off the sea, and the sun was warm on her face. She watched Quin bend down to pat Riley as he took the stick again, and her heart gave an unexpected little twist. It was all too perfect. Could it even be real? And if it was real, how could anything this sweet really last? Quin threw the stick and came over and sat down beside her.

"I'm planning a little dinner party for Saturday," announced Kestra. "Just Holly and Matthew actually, and Page and me." She turned to Page, "Hey, do you think your mom would want to join us?"

"I can check and see."

"Great." She turned back to Quin. "So, how about it? The first meal from that fabulous kitchen."

"So you think a great kitchen guarantees a great meal?" he asked with a grin.

"Well, maybe you'd better eat one of your delicious microwave meals before you come!" She jabbed him with her elbow playfully.

"Like I said, I happen to like Cajun food. Blackened catfish, blackened salmon, blackened whatever, I'm game. I'll give it a try."

"Hopefully, we won't be having Cajun! Thanks for the tea. Now it's back to work."

She and Page spent the rest of the day cleaning the kitchen and dining area and getting it ready to move things into. Kestra decided to go ahead and set up a table and chairs in the dining room, and perhaps even a few things in the library. After all, this was her house, there was no reason she couldn't start using rooms that weren't being worked on. She called Holly that night to see if she knew any high-school boys who wanted to make a few bucks moving furniture and boxes the next day. Holly offered to check with her sister who had teens.

The next morning, a work crew of three high-school boys

came over to help. One was Holly's nephew, Nathan, and the other two were friends of his.

"Hi, Nathan, I bet you don't even remember me," said Kestra. "The last time I saw you, you weren't even in kindergarten."

The six-foot-plus teen grinned. "Yeah, I remember you. You used to help Aunt Holly baby-sit me and my sister. I always thought you were real nice."

"Well, thanks. It's sure great to have you guys here to help. This is Page. You may know her from school."

Page smiled shyly and Kestra suddenly realized how different this Page looked compared to the sultry girl she'd met in the coffee shop just last month.

"I sort of remember you," said Nathan. "You're new in town, aren't you?"

"Yeah, we just moved over after spring break."

Nathan introduced his two friends, and it looked like the four teens were hitting it off okay. Kestra handed Page the list they had made yesterday. "Page is in charge since she knows where everything is and where it all goes. I'll stay in the house and try to get things put away as you bring them in. Good luck, troops! Lunch will be at twelve o'clock sharp."

They worked like an army all morning. Kestra couldn't believe how quickly the house transformed as pieces of furniture were placed here and there. It was amazing how the antiques went perfectly with the house. She longed for Quin to stop by and see the progress. She wanted to hear his opinion on whether the leather couch looked too modern for the library, or if the antique desk and craftsman-style lamp helped to make it fit in. Maybe she should toss a plaid blanket across the back of the sofa. Maybe she should call Holly and see if she had any tapestry pillows, nothing too frilly of course, but perhaps something with hunting dogs or horses. It was such fun making the house look homey.

The kitchen was coming along nicely. She had gotten three boxes of plates unloaded onto the overhead shelves. Holly had tried to convince her that the cupboards needed doors, but Kestra knew from experience that plates should be within quick reach in a restaurant, so she had opted for open shelves. She stepped back and admired the neat stacks of china and knew she'd made the right choice. Finally it was getting close to noon, so she made herself stop unpacking boxes and begin putting a lunch together. She knew the moving crew would be hungry. She made big submarine sandwiches and poured a bag of chips into a bowl. She'd gotten a couple of pounds of red potato salad from the deli yesterday, and she set a selection of sodas on the counter just as the four carried in a bunch of chairs to go around the long sturdy harvest table that she had chosen to go in the dining room for now.

"Good, I'm glad to see you brought your own chairs," she called from the kitchen. "Help yourself to lunch. The bathroom's down the hall there. Please excuse the mess, I haven't gotten back that far to clean yet."

"Hey, we found an extra pair of hands," called Page. "And we promised him lunch if he helped out."

Quin set down two chairs and grinned at her. "You know me, never could refuse a good home-cooked meal."

"Well, you're more than welcome to join the crew. Can you believe the progress we're making?" She set a bowl of fresh fruit on the table.

"It's starting to look like someone really lives here. I can even see the walls starting to smile."

"Yeah, I know what you mean."

Soon the six of them were seated around the long table, with Quin at one end and Kestra at the other.

"Would you like me to ask a blessing?" offered Quin quietly.

"That'd be great." She glanced around at the teens, wondering if that would make them feel uncomfortable, but they had already bowed their heads.

"Dear Lord, we thank you for the food that you have provided us, and for the one who prepared it. Even more than that, we thank you for this house, The Wise Man's House. We pray your blessing for Kestra as she lives here, that you continue to show her how to build her life upon you the same way that the wise man built his house upon the rock. Amen."

She looked up and wiped a tear from her eye. "Thanks, Quin." The others were already digging in as her eyes locked with his across the long table. He smiled, and she wondered if she would ever be able to live without him.

~ 29 ~

Friday finally came, and with it the horses. Page worked all morning, making certain the stalls were perfectly safe and secure. She even checked the fence line and made sure there were no dangers within the long strip of overgrown pasture. When Hank pulled in with his long horse trailer, it looked like Page was walking several inches off the ground. Kestra tried not to get in the way as Page and Quin helped Hank unload the nervous horses from the trailer.

Othello was the first one out, and it was a good thing because he looked like he hadn't enjoyed the ride much. Quin led the agitated horse out to the open gate and released him in the pasture. Before long the others joined him. It was plain to see that Page loved all four horses. She proclaimed them all to be perfect, but she appeared to be drawn to the older horse, the one that Kestra had rescued from an uncertain fate. Hank told them that the old mare's name was Lady and that she'd been quite a horse in her day.

Page helped Hank drag out a couple of bales of alfalfa and a bag of oats. She listened carefully as he instructed her as to the care and feeding of the animals. Kestra was certain these horses were going to be in very good hands.

"Now, before you go and ride them down that trail to the beach, I'd suggest that you lead them up and down it a couple of times till they get the hang of it," said Hank as he surveyed the slightly steep trail. "They should have no problem once they're used to it, but I'd give them a chance to get the feel for it without someone in the saddle."

Kestra wrote out a check and thanked Hank for all his help.

"You just call if you have any questions," said Hank. He looked out to the pasture and sniffed, and Kestra knew this wasn't easy for him.

"Say, Hank, if you ever want to come take a ride, you'd be more than welcome."

He tipped his hat. "Now that might be right nice. Maybe I could bring the Misses over here for supper once you get your restaurant going, and we could take a ride on the beach. Yep, that'd be right nice. Thank you very much."

Even before Hank pulled his trailer out of the driveway, Page was saddling up Lady.

"Well, how about it?" said Quin. "Should we lead them down to the beach and get them used to the trail, maybe take a little ride?"

"Sure, but you'll have to help me with the saddle," said Kestra. "It looks quite different from English."

It was a cool foggy day, and Kestra decided to run back to the house for a sweater. Riley followed her. She told him to stay in the house, promising that she would take him out with the horses later on, but for now they had to get them used to the trail slowly. He looked up with trusting eyes as if he understood.

On her way past the carriage house, she remembered spying her old English riding helmet on top of a box. She dashed in and picked it up. She wasn't ready for another concussion. By the time she returned, three horses were saddled and ready to go. Quin had decided to take Chip on this first run, then take Othello down later.

They carefully led them down the trail with no problem. Once on the beach, Quin gave Kestra a few tips and helped her into the saddle.

"Now, I want you to take it nice and easy," he warned. "It's only been a few days since your fall. Helmet or not, I don't think that pretty head of yours can take another blow."

She smiled. "Sure, I'll take it easy." Then she gave Annie a quick nudge, and they took off in a slow trot. Kestra had never enjoyed the up and down motion of trotting, so she gave Annie another nudge, and the horse broke into a smooth gallop. Kestra hunched over and leaned into the horse, feeling the smooth gate and settling into the motion. Much better. Annie headed easily down the open beach, and Kestra was sure that she and Annie were going to be friends for a long time. She soon passed Page on Lady and waved. She had almost forgotten how great it was to ride, how alive it made her feel!

Soon she heard the sound of hooves pounding from behind her, but she kept her gaze straight ahead. She sensed the other horse pull up beside and could see with her peripheral vision that it was Quin on Chip. She glanced his way and saw deep lines of worry carved in his forehead, and immediately reined Annie to a trot and then a walk.

"What's wrong?" she asked breathlessly, looking over her shoulder. "Is Page okay?"

"She's fine. I just wanted to make sure that everything's under control here. You weren't having a problem with Annie were you?" He asked with a slightly sheepish look. "I thought maybe she was running away with you. But it looks like you know what you're doing."

"Thanks." Kestra kept herself from smiling. His concern was

really very sweet, even if it wasn't necessary. "Yes, I think Annie and I are going to get along just fine."

Page joined them and they walked the horses up to the jetty and stopped for a while.

"Now, this is the way to live," said Page. "Kestra, I'll bet your restaurant will really take off when people find out you have horses! I mean, people should be glad to drive from Portland for a chance to have a beach ride, and then they'll be so hungry, they won't even care if the food's very good or not."

Kestra smirked at Page. "Thanks a lot! But for your information, the food is going to be good! After all, I might even get your mom to be my chef."

"Oh, that's right," laughed Page. "I forgot."

"And for that, I am going to beat you back to the trail." Kestra climbed into the saddle and took off, with Quin and Page right behind her. Quin quickly passed her, and to her dismay, so did Page. Then she remembered how Hank had said that Annie was a good horse, but not too fast.

"That's okay, girl," she patted Annie as they slowed down before they reached the trail. "I'm not looking for a racehorse."

The next morning, Kestra and Page busily cleaned and got things ready for the dinner party, though Page took plenty of breaks to go check on the horses. Karen had agreed to come for dinner, but only if she could help prepare it. She arrived unexpectedly at noon with several bags of groceries and big plans. She explained that she wanted to prove to Kestra first hand what a great chef she'd make for the restaurant, and finally Kestra agreed to let Karen take over. Actually, it was a relief; plus it allowed Kestra to do what she really loved best, getting the house all fixed up for a dinner party. She made a run to town to pick up fresh flowers and popped into Holly's shop for a quick look around as well.

"I'm so glad you stopped," said Holly, pulling out a big cardboard box. "Look what just came in yesterday!" Kestra peeked in the box to see tapestry pillows almost exactly like she had described to Holly by phone, as well as some burgundy candles and a beautiful vase.

"These are perfect! I can't wait to see how this looks in the library! I was thinking we could have coffee and dessert in there." Kestra glanced out the window and spotted a fog bank sitting on the horizon. "And maybe it will get cool enough this evening to make a small fire. It will be so cozy in there with a fire!"

"I can't wait to see how the place looks," said Holly eagerly. "Mom's coming over at four, and Matthew and I will head over early for that beach ride that you promised. I told Matthew to come prepared for a ride and to bring a change of clothes if he wanted to clean up afterwards. I know I plan to clean up afterwards. I even got a new dress."

"Great! This is going to be such fun! See you later." Kestra hadn't even thought about what she was going to wear. But she decided to pick something out first thing when she got home. No more last minute wardrobe disasters like the last dinner with Quin!

Back at home, she quickly arranged flowers, putting several pretty bouquets around the house. She placed her new cushions on the couch in the library and stuck the burgundy candles in her antique brass candleholders, situating them carefully on the restored mantle. She even laid a little stack of kindling by the fireplace, just in case. Then she went up and looked through her closet. Finally, after tossing aside several dresses, she decided there were no rules that said she must wear a dress. It was an old habit she had acquired with Jack. Whenever they went out, he had always insisted upon skirts and heels. At last, she picked out an outfit she had gotten on her latest trip to Seattle. It had been one of those impulse buys, but she'd never had an occasion to wear it. She laid out a pair of nice jeans just about the color of an eggplant, then pulled out the matching silk brocade blouse and held it up. It was a gorgeous blouse, and she could just imagine how nice it would look in the firelight.

Matthew and Holly arrived before five. Page already had the two mares saddled, and Quin was working on Othello by the time Kestra led them out to the stable.

"Hello there, cowpokes!" called Kestra. Quin slapped the dust off his hands and came over to meet Matthew.

"I've heard a lot about you," said Quin. "Nice to finally put a face to the name."

"Same here," said Matthew. "These are some good-looking ponies you got here, Kestra." He ran his hand down Chip's back. "Can I give you a hand, Page?" Matthew went over and relieved her of the heavy saddle and tossed it onto Chip's back.

Kestra explained how they still needed to walk the horses down the trail, and then they all headed out one by one. Quin led the way with Othello, since he knew this horse didn't like to follow the others. And soon they were all down on the beach.

A stiff breeze began to whip up and that bank of fog quickly rolled in. The cool weather made the horses frisky, and even Annie was feeling her oats. They ran the horses right up to the water's edge, but Othello was being difficult. Quin told them he'd meet them at the jetty and took off. Kestra felt a small wave of fear as she watched the powerful horse snort and throw his head back, but Quin appeared to be in control.

By the time the other three reached the jetty, the entire beach was blanketed in thick wet fog. Quin had already dismounted in one piece, and tied Othello to a large driftwood log. They did likewise, and Holly and Matthew took off climbing onto the rocks of the jetty. Kestra started to follow, but noticed that Quin was lingering back.

"I think I better stay with the horses. Othello is being a bit unpredictable today. You go on ahead, if you like."

She turned and smiled. "I'm sure they won't mind if I don't join them." Actually, she was thinking she'd rather be alone with Quin.

"They both seem very nice," said Quin as he sat down on a log and wiped off a place beside him for her.

"You sound relieved."

"Well, I wasn't too sure about this Matthew fellow. It seemed I'd heard his name connected to Dan so often, and I began to think—"

She cut him off with laughter. "Dan and Matthew are as different as night and day!"

"I can see that now." He glanced up at the two on the jetty. Matthew was leaning over and giving Holly a hand. "They seem to like each other a lot. Is it serious?"

"Holly is hoping it is. But Matthew is a widower, and Holly thinks he's being cautious. He lost both his wife and son, and I think Holly's a little worried that she won't measure up."

He nodded. "It can be hard."

"You say that like you've had experience." She hoped he wasn't thinking about Jack. Surely he knew that he had nothing to compete with in that regard.

"No, not really." He looked at her. "Funny that you never ask thoug...."

She felt her cheeks grow warm. He was right, she never had asked about the possibility of other loves in his life. Of course, a handsome man like him could not have made it to this stage of life without some romantic involvement. Perhaps he had even been married. The thought staggered her. She had never even imagined it before. She turned and looked at him as if seeing him for the first time.

"You're wondering..." He spoke quietly, looking intently

into her eyes. "But you still won't ask."

She swallowed hard and looked away. She stared out at the sea. It was several shades of gray, almost like a black and white photo might look. A gull swooped down and cried a long haunting cry. What if there was someone else in his life right now?

"Is it because you like keeping me a mystery man? Does that allow your imagination to make me into whatever you might like me to be? Perfect and noble. No faults. A phantom lover."

"No," she answered quickly. Too quickly.

"It's easier to fall in love with a fantasy, you know."

That was twice that he'd used the word love. She looked at him uneasily. She knew if they crossed this bridge there would be no turning back for her. She already knew that she loved him. If they talked about their relationship, she wouldn't be able to keep her feelings inside. And if she let them out, there was the chance that he wouldn't feel the same. And then it would all end. Her perfect world would be shattered.

He reached over and took her cold hands into his. She looked up at his face. "Kestra, I want you to know me. I want you to ask me any questions that you like. I'm tired of being a mystery man to you."

"What do you mean?"

"I have to admit that at first I liked it. Keeping the distance, getting to know you without having to disclose myself. It was really quite appealing. You see, it wasn't too long ago that I came out of a relationship with a woman that was—well, let's just say it was very disappointing. In fact, in some ways she loved me just the same way that Jack loved you. She loved the image of me—who she thought I was, or maybe who she thought I should be. I appreciate that you seem to accept me as I am. You respect my need for privacy. You've seen the hermit side of me and haven't questioned it. You're content to sit quietly with me, or even chatter in that cheerful way, without getting much response from me. I like that. It's very comfortable. Very comforting."

"So what's wrong then?"

"Nothing's wrong. But I'm worried that you don't seem to want to know about my past, who I really am."

"I do want to know. It's just that I've gotten so—so comfortable living in the present. Sometimes, I almost forget that we both had lives before this. And maybe deep down, I'm worried that you do have some horrible dark secrets that will ruin all this." She forced herself to laugh.

He squeezed her hand. "Well, if you really think that I could be hiding some awful secret, then you are either very trusting to have let me into your life, or else you're just plain foolish."

"Hey, you two," called Holly with a bright smile. "We've worked up quite an appetite."

Kestra pulled her hands away and stood. She didn't like the fact that Quin had suggested she might be foolish.

"Well, what are you waiting for," called Kestra, climbing into the saddle. "Last one back is a rotten egg!" She nudged Annie and took off.

Page met them at the stable and helped Quin put the horses away, while the other three headed back to the house.

"Something is smelling mighty good in here," said Matthew as they entered the house. "Wow, this place is looking very nice. What a transformation!"

"Kestra, it's gorgeous!" Holly dashed from room to room all around the downstairs inspecting every single square inch.

"It looks pretty good as long as you don't go past the dining room into the south wing. It's still a disaster over there." Kestra pulled off her sweater and stuck her head in the kitchen. "Looking good, Karen. Need any help?"

"Not on your life. Page said she would be back to help after she puts the horses up. Now, you folks better go get cleaned up, and then there will be hors d'oeuvres in the library."

"Karen, I think you're hired," called Kestra.

"Don't decide yet. You know what they say about the proof being in the pudding…"

Kestra pointed Matthew to a spare room to freshen up, and Holly joined her in her bedroom.

"What a pretty dress, Holly," said Kestra as Holly slipped a long sleeveless paisley dress over her head.

"Thanks, but there's no time for small talk. Tell me just how serious you and Quin are. It almost looked like he was proposing when we walked up. I hope we didn't interrupt anything."

"No, of course not. Although we were having a pretty heavy discussion."

"About what?"

"Oh, I don't know. I think our relationship is about to go to a deeper level." Kestra pulled on her jeans.

"Is that good? You don't sound too excited. Do you want him to slow down?"

"No, I'm very excited. I guess I'm just scared. I mean I know how I feel about him, but what if he doesn't feel that way?"

"Looked to me like he's feeling pretty serious."

"He was telling me that I don't really know him."

"And?"

"Well, he made it sound as if I don't want to really know him, like I'm in love with who I think he is. You know, my mystery man." Kestra slowly buttoned her blouse and tucked it in.

"Is it true?"

"No, I feel like I know him."

"Do you know anything more about his past?"

"Not really." Kestra stared at herself in the mirror. Maybe Quin was right, maybe she was just foolish.

Holly grabbed Kestra by the shoulders and turned her towards her. "Listen, girl, there's nothing to be afraid of. Quin seems like a good guy. Go ahead, get to know him. Find out who he is, where he's been. If it doesn't feel right, you can just step away, you can cut it off."

Kestra sank into the chair. "I don't think it would be that easy. Holly, I'm almost certain that I love him so much that even if he were a convicted felon, I wouldn't be able to walk away."

Holly laughed. "Don't be silly. He's not a felon!"

Kestra started to giggle, too. "Of course not! I guess I'm just getting nervous about taking the big plunge here."

"Well, speaking as one who has just taken it, jump in, the water's fine!"

"What do you mean?"

Holly held out her left hand to display a glistening diamond ring.

"You're kidding!" shrieked Kestra. "I can't believe this!" She gave Holly a big hug, then stood back and stared in wonder. "Well, congratulations! When did this happen?"

"Out on the jetty!"

"Oh, Holly, I'm so happy for you! Hey, this dinner is a real celebration. An engagement party!"

They joined the men downstairs in the library. Quin had lit the fire, and he and Matthew were already munching on mini crab cakes and smoked salmon paté.

"It looks like a gentlemen's gathering," teased Holly. "The only thing missing is a couple of good cigars." She went up to Matthew and was welcomed with a hug.

"And one other thing is missing," said Kestra as she left the room and hurried to the kitchen. Before long, she unearthed a bottle of sparkling cider and some champagne glasses.

"Come with me, Karen and Page," she said. "We have some toasting to do." She led them back to the library and passed around glasses and filled them one by one, finally turning to Holly and Matthew.

"Congratulations, you two," she said, raising her glass high. "On your new engagement and upcoming marriage!"

They all cheered and toasted them.

"Now, you and Kestra can really plan that wedding," said Page. Matthew looked quizzically at them, and Holly grinned.

"Oh, you know how girls talk," Page said, and everyone laughed.

They moved on to the dinner table which looked perfect. Karen outdid herself with a fabulous meal of Caesar salad, duck à l'orange, and brussel sprouts with chestnuts. The flavors and presentation were amazing. Everyone paid the highest compliments to the chef, and Kestra officially offered her the job in front of witnesses. Finally, they finished the last course and returned to the library to relax. The big log Quin had thrown on the fire was burning nicely now, and it appeared that Page had slipped in and lit the candles, giving the room a warm cozy glow.

They had just settled into a friendly flow of conversation when they heard a loud knocking at the door.

"How about if I get that," offered Quin, rising from the sofa. Kestra nodded, then turned back to Holly to return to discussing wedding ideas. Suddenly an angry commotion interrupted them.

"I wanna see the woman of the house!" yelled a slurred voice that sounded familiar. "Lemme in! I gotta see Kestra!"

"I think you better stay out here, Dan," said Quin in a calm but firm voice.

"Don't you go telling me what to do, you lazy, good-for-nothin—" There was a loud crash and everyone ran to the hallway to see.

⤙ 30 ⤚

Kestra stared in disbelief at Dan's face, twisted with hatred and what looked like the effects of too much alcohol. It reminded her of her father's drunken rages and filled her with horror. A vase was shattered across the slate floor, and Quin held Dan back with both hands on his chest.

"Git outta my way you lousy—" Dan pulled back and took a wild swing at Quin, but Quin ducked. Then Dan lunged towards Quin, knocking them both to the floor with Dan on top. Just as Dan drew back a clenched fist ready to strike, Matthew grabbed his arm and peeled him off Quin. Matthew then dragged Dan kicking and yelling toward the front door.

"Don't worry," Matthew called over his shoulder. "I'll try to talk some sense into him!"

Kestra ran over to check on Quin. His upper arm was bleeding from where he had fallen on a sharp shard of broken pottery.

"You're bleeding, Quin! Are you okay?"

He sat up. "I'm fine. Just a cut."

"Come in the kitchen and let's take a look," commanded Karen. It took all three women to push him into the kitchen. By then Page joined them.

"I can call the police and have them come haul Dan away," she offered. "I always knew he was no good!"

"I don't think that's necessary, Page," said Holly. "But I'll go check and make sure everything's okay. Matthew can probably get him to calm down."

"Off with the shirt," commanded Karen, grabbing a clean tea towel from the drawer. Quin made no move to remove his shirt, so Kestra began undoing the buttons. Her fingers trembled nervously when she saw his dark hairy chest exposed. She looked up apologetically and saw that he was grinning.

"Doesn't look like he's in too much pain," joked Page as Kestra and Karen peeled the blood-soaked shirt from his shoulder.

"Oh, my," said Karen as she quickly placed the towel on the bleeding wound. "That's going to need some serious stitches. We better get you to town right away."

Kestra's hands were shaking and her knees felt weak. "I don't think I better drive."

"I'll drive him in to town, as long as you don't mind my old beater car," offered Karen calmly. "It's time for Page and me to go home anyway. Kestra, you guys can arrange some way to get him back home after things calm down around here. Let's take him out the back way, Page. That way we won't meet Dan."

Kestra ran and grabbed the blanket from the couch and threw it over Quin's bare shoulders. She looked into his eyes, wanting to say something meaningful, but could think of nothing.

"Don't worry, Kestra. It's really nothing," he assured her.

"I'm so sorry," she said. And then they were gone.

She sat down in the library and waited. And she prayed. First she prayed for Quin, then she prayed for Dan. As angry as she was at Dan, she also felt sorry for him. Why was he acting like this? She could hear Matthew and Holly talking to Dan outside. Every once in a while, Dan's voice would raise in a fitful rage, then Matthew would subdue him.

Finally, the front door opened and Holly came in.

"Matthew wants to drive Dan home. He's certainly in no condition to be on the road. Matthew asked me to check on how Quin is before we go."

"Karen and Page are taking him to the emergency room to have his arm stitched up."

"Oh, it must have been bad."

Kestra nodded then burst into tears. Holly held her for a moment and stroked her hair. "Everything will be okay, Kestra. Remember, all things work together for good for those who love God and try to do his will—or something like that. And this will work for good, too, Kestra. Just wait."

"I hope you're right."

Holly went back outside, and Kestra heard Dan's truck take off. She ran to the door to see if Dan was behind the wheel and was met by Holly. "It's okay, Matthew's driving. He told me to stay with you and that he'll swing by the hospital and pick up Quin."

"What an angel!" said Kestra.

"Don't I know it," Holly answered wistfully.

"I'm so sorry we ruined your engagement night."

"It's not your fault, silly. And—" she held out her hand and looked at the ring again, "the important thing is that it really, really, happened!"

They finished cleaning up the kitchen, then Kestra called the hospital to check on Quin. The nurse had no information about him and offered to give him a message. But Kestra couldn't think of anything to say. She told the nurse not to bother.

She and Holly went back to the library and Kestra tossed

another log on the fire. They chatted for a while, but soon they both sat silently listening to the mantle clock slowly ticking. Riley came up and wagged his tail expectantly.

"Do you need to go out, boy?" asked Kestra, eager for a distraction. She took him outside and walked down the driveway toward the cottage. Suddenly, she thought of Dan and felt uneasy. She knew he was probably safe at home by now and that Matthew had his truck, but for some reason she no longer felt completely safe.

"Come on, Riley," she called into the dark night. "Let's go back inside." Back in the house, she heard Holly talking on the phone. It sounded like it must be Matthew on the other end.

"What's happening?" asked Kestra when Holly hung up.

"Matthew's with Quin at the hospital, and it will probably be a couple of hours before they can stitch him up. I guess there was a bad accident on the highway with this fog. But Matthew said Quin's just fine, and everything looks okay. He told me either to drive his car home or to spend the night if you need company. He said not to wait up."

Kestra was glad for Holly's company. They stayed up until after midnight, but finally they decided to go to bed. Kestra tried to stay alert to hear the men drive up, but she didn't awake until midmorning.

Her first impulse was to run and check on Quin, but then she decided he might need to sleep in after his late night in the hospital.

They decided it was too late to make it to church, and Holly left just before noon. Kestra waved good-bye to Holly, then walked over to the cottage to see how Quin was doing. She knocked on the door and waited. There was no answer. Maybe he was still sleeping. She tiptoed away and checked on the horses, then took Riley down to the beach for a quick run.

When she returned, she was sure he must be up. She

knocked again, but still there was no answer. She walked around to the side and noticed that his Land Rover was gone. That seemed odd, but then maybe he was just fine, like Holly had said.

She went back to the house, telling herself that Quin was fine. He had probably gone into town to get a paper and maybe some of those cinnamon rolls that he liked from the bakery. Maybe she should learn how to make them herself. She had just pulled out a cookbook and started to look for a good cinnamon roll recipe when Riley began barking as if someone was at the door. Maybe that was Quin now!

She ran to the door and pulled it open, then stared in shock. It was Dan! She started to close it, but he stopped it with his boot.

"Kestra, wait," he pleaded. "I'm sorry. I just came over to apologize. I can't believe what I did last night. And I won't be surprised if you never speak to me again, but I'm sorry."

She fought to find her voice. "It's okay, Dan. I understand, you didn't mean to do that, you were drunk..."

He looked down. "I really am sorry, Kestra. Can you please forgive me?"

"Yes," she swallowed. She knew it was good for him to say these things, but it was hard hearing him like this.

"Can I come in and talk to you?"

Suddenly she recalled how his face looked last night, the anger and rage, the hatred...

"I don't think so, Dan. Not right now."

He removed his foot from the door and turned away, walking slowly back to his truck. Was she wrong? Should she let him in? She started to call out when she remembered what Quin had said about not trusting him. She closed the door and prayed.

It was the longest day. She kept watching, hoping to see

Quin drive up, and at the same time watching in fear to see that Dan didn't. She wished it weren't Sunday, then at least Page would be here.

Finally, in the late evening she took Riley and walked over to the cottage once more. It was dark and she was sure he wasn't there. But by now, she was more than concerned, she was worried. She tried the door. It was locked. Now that was strange, she had never seen him lock the door. She stood on the porch, wondering what to do. Should she go get her key and let herself in? Suddenly Riley began to growl as if an intruder were nearby. It was a moonless night, and she could see nothing.

"Come on, boy," she called as she took off toward the lights of her house. Soon they were safe inside. But for some reason her house did not feel safe. She told herself it was ridiculous, but her heart kept pounding with fear just the same. She ran from door to door, locking everything tight. She even locked the windows. Finally, she took Riley upstairs and barricaded herself in her bedroom. She picked up the phone to call Holly, but only got her machine. She left a lame message, then fell to her knees.

"Dear God, please take away this fear. I trust you to take care of me. My life is in your hands. And please, God, wherever Quin is, please take care of him, too." She crawled into bed and went to sleep.

She was so glad to see Page the next morning. She went with her to the stable to check on the horses and helped let them out and fill the water trough. She told Page about Quin's strange disappearance, trying to sound nonchalant.

"You mean he left without even telling you?" asked Page as she closed the gate to the pasture.

"Yes, I thought it was a little strange."

"Seems pretty strange to me. It doesn't sound like Quin. Are you sure he's not in some kind of danger? I mean, Dan was so mad, do you think Dan could have done anything to Quin?"

Kestra made herself laugh. "No, of course not. Dan may be jealous, but he's not a criminal."

"How can you be so sure? Haven't you ever heard that the worst crimes are crimes of passion?" Page looked at her intensely.

"I'm sure there's some logical explanation."

"Maybe, but don't you owe it to Quin to at least go check his place out and make sure that everything looks okay? Like, last night I was watching this movie, and this lady was—well I won't go into the details, but she was all tied up and no one came to find her—"

"Enough, Page! I'm going to get the key right now. I'll meet you there!" She started to run and called over her shoulder. "And besides, you shouldn't watch such horrible movies!"

By the time she reached the cottage she was breathless, but she knew it was more from fear than exertion. She prayed a wordless prayer and unlocked the door. They both stepped inside, then Page gasped. There on the floor was a bloody shirt.

"Oh, that's the shirt he was wearing when he got hurt, Page. Remember?" Kestra walked into the front room and looked around. Nothing looked disturbed. It was a little messy, but then that was normal. She looked for his lap-top computer, but didn't see it.

"Let's check the bedroom," said Page, pushing open the door and stepping back quickly as if she expected someone to leap out. The room looked normal, the bed was made. Kestra looked under the bed. She had noticed his suitcase under there the day she had recovered from her fall.

"His suitcase is gone," said Kestra.

"Did he say he was going somewhere?"

"No." Kestra looked around, hoping for some clue. Nothing really seemed to spell foul play. But it just didn't make sense that he would leave without telling her.

"Well, I think it's fishy." Page began looking around, opening drawers and moving things.

"Page, we can't go snooping around. We have no right. Quin's a grown man—if he wants to take off without telling anyone, it's his own business."

"But I thought you guys had something going—"

"Obviously not enough to check in with me regarding his whereabouts!" Kestra didn't mean to snap at her, but she was on the verge of tears.

"I'm sorry, Kestra."

"It's okay. Let's get out of here."

The mail truck was parked in front of her house when they came around the driveway.

"I was just about to give up," called the postman. "Got a registered letter for Ms. Kestra McKenzie."

"That's me," said Kestra running over to see. Maybe it was from Quin.

"Sign here."

She signed, and he tore off the slip, handed her the envelope, and climbed back into his truck. She eagerly tore it open and looked inside.

"What is it?" asked Page.

"It looks like a bill." Kestra flipped it over and read the letterhead. "Dan Hackett Construction," she read out loud. "Just great. He's got a lot of nerve to bill me before he's even finished. Holy cow!"

"What is it?"

Kestra walked toward the porch. It felt like her legs were about to give way. She collapsed on the steps and looked at the bottom figure again. "Page, come read this to me. I think I'm seeing things!"

Page came over and looked, reading the number by Kestra's

finger out loud. "Gee, I didn't think anyone really had that kind of money. You must really be rich, Kestra."

Kestra shook her head. "It must be a mistake."

"Kestra, are you okay? You're face is as white as a sheet."

"I guess I'm in shock." She forced her eyes to focus on the figure again. It must be wrong! Or maybe that was the amount for the entire completed project. Even in that case, it was incredibly high. Whatever the case, she would put a stop to his work this instant!

She ran into the house and called his number. She knew it by heart and expected to get his answering machine. She was disappointed when she got him in person.

"Dan, I just got your bill." She willed herself to stay in control. "I think there must be some mistake. The figure is way too high. Is that supposed to be for the entire job?"

"No, that's for the work that's been done to date."

"Then I want you to stop work immediately on this house."

"But we're not done—"

"I don't care. The rest will have to wait. The fact is, Dan, I don't have that much money. I'm sure you must have figured it wrong. That amount is twice what I paid for the entire house!"

"I can double-check, Kestra. But I'm sure that it's right."

"Then you'd better double-check. And I expect you to get back to me right away."

"I'll get right to it. I'm sorry if it's upsetting. But I told you in the beginning that this was a costly project—"

"You never told me anything like these kinds of numbers!" She hung up. She knew it was childish, but she was so upset she couldn't think straight.

Page handed her a glass of lemonade. "Here, Kestra. Calm down, okay. Everything is going to be okay. Remember what you told me about this being God's house?"

Kestra nodded meekly and took a sip.

"Well, then God can take care of it, right?"

"You're right, Page." Kestra's voice was barely more than a whisper. "Thanks."

Page smiled. "It's going to be okay. Just wait. I'll bet he calls back and says he put too many zeroes in it."

"I sure hope so, Page. Either that or I'm out of business before I even start."

~ *31* ~

Kestra decided to work in the house for the rest of the day, just in case the phone rang. She asked Page to hunt down the despised answering machine; it was about time she set it up.

After an hour of sanding the dining room floor, she realized there must be a better way. At this rate she'd still be sanding by Christmas. Maybe there was some sort of machine she could rent. She sat up and brushed the fine sawdust from her hands. She was coated in it. Just then, the jangling telephone jerked her to her feet. She picked it up hoping to hear Quin's voice, telling her that he was okay. Instead it was Dan.

"Well, Kestra, I've checked my numbers, and the figure I quoted is correct. Is that a problem?"

"Of course it's a problem. Dan, it's outrageous! Can you explain why it's so high."

"Well, you know, Kestra, you've asked for a lot of changes. Now, take that kitchen, we had it all worked out for one way, and then you went and got all that stuff in Portland. And then there's all those antique fixtures you insisted on using. It all adds up, you know."

She took a breath. "I just can't believe it could add up to so much. Are you absolutely sure?"

"Positive. In fact, I already tried to cut you some slack. I'm probably losing money on this job."

"Really?"

"Yep, but since we're friends and all, I was willing to let some of my fees go..."

She could think of nothing to say. Was he telling the truth? Should she trust him? What choice did she have? She felt sick inside. She wondered what Jack would think if he could know how she had managed to blow everything he had left to her already. "Thanks, Dan," she said weakly. "I'll have to get back to you. But the work will have to stop. I can't afford anymore—"

"But can you afford this?" he asked quickly.

"No, I can't afford this. I don't know what I'm going to do, Dan. Any suggestions?" She tried to keep the sarcasm out of her voice.

"Well, I'd hate to do it, but you know we have a contract..."

"Hate to do what?"

"Place a lien."

"A lien?"

"Well, I've got people to pay, too. You can't expect folks to work without pay. That's not very Christian of you—"

"I never said I wouldn't pay anything, I just said I don't have this much. I'm willing to make a very large payment. That should certainly keep the wolf from your door." This time the sarcasm was obvious, and she didn't care.

"Well, a payment would be nice, but if you can't pay in full, we've got us a pretty serious problem, Kestra."

She wished she could see his face. It was almost like she could hear him smiling, almost as if this were some kind of cat and mouse game and he finally had her where he wanted her.

"Well then, I guess we have a pretty serious problem, Dan."

She hung up and broke into sobs.

"I found the answering machine—" Page came over and put her hand on Kestra's back. "Are you okay?"

Kestra lifted up her head. "Well, my contractor has put a lien on my house, and the man I love has walked out of my life. Everything's just peachy."

The phone rang again. This time it was Holly. Before Holly could get a word in, Kestra told her the whole horrible story.

"Kestra, that's awful about Dan. But I do have a bit of good news about Quin—"

"What? What? Tell me—"

"He called and left a message on my machine. He tried to reach you yesterday morning from the airport, but you were out. He said that he had to leave for some business. His shoulder is fine, not to worry, and he'll be in touch."

Kestra sighed. "Thanks, Holly. I'm just about to hook up my answering machine. Did he say what kind of business?"

"No, but it sounded like he was in good spirits."

"Well, I'm glad someone is."

"Now, remember Kestra, you have always said that it is God's house—"

"I know, I know. And those words are coming back to haunt me now. I just hope God can afford it."

Holly laughed. "I think he can. You just need to do what you can and then trust him."

"Thanks, Holly. I'll try."

Kestra stayed up late trying to figure a way to make ends meet. She could sell her car. Sell the horses. Try to finish up the rest of the work herself. Maybe take in boarders... But no matter how she tried, it just never seemed to add up to enough. Had this whole idea been a big mistake? Had she bitten off more than she could chew?

The week passed slowly, and still Kestra heard nothing from

Quin. She began to wonder if he'd left for good. Maybe all that business with Dan was just too much. Quin had been attacked in his own home, and then again in hers. She couldn't really blame him for not wanting to become part of this mess.

Kestra had told Page on Monday that she could no longer afford to pay her to work, but Page wanted to continue to care for the horses in trade for riding. Kestra didn't tell her she would probably have to sell her horses, but she figured Page must suspect as much. Kestra could see that Page was doing more than just the horses, but she didn't mention it.

Holly called Thursday morning and invited Kestra to come to Bible study, and as much as Kestra wanted to, she declined out of fear that she might come face-to-face with Dan.

On Saturday, Kestra was awakened by several cars pulling into the driveway. She quickly pulled on clothes, then looked out the window to see Karen and Page, Holly and Matthew, along with Nathan and his two friends. Another car pulled up and out climbed several other members of the Bible study group. Everyone had on work clothes and carried some sort of tools.

"We're your emergency crew," explained Karen. "We thought we could help get that dining room and south wing done so you could start up your business, and then maybe I can come work for you. And you can start making some money off this establishment."

"I can't believe it," stammered Kestra. "This is so sweet."

Matthew took the lead, sending everyone off to various jobs—painting, sanding, and repairing. Karen took charge of feeding the crew, and they all worked harder than any crew Kestra had ever seen Dan lead. It was amazing all they had accomplished by the end of the day. The south wing was actually beginning to look like there might be hope after all.

"With food like this, you might be able to talk us into coming again next Saturday," offered Nathan as they all sat outside eating.

"I'm game," said Karen and everyone else chimed in.

Holly and Matthew stayed after the others had left.

"I asked Dan about the amount of the bill," said Matthew. "He nicely told me it was none of my business."

"Thanks, anyway," said Kestra.

"He hasn't been to church or Bible study for the last two weeks. But we're still praying for him," said Holly.

"I know it really isn't any of my business, Kestra," began Matthew, and then he stopped.

"What is it?" asked Kestra.

"Well, keep in mind, I'm not recommending this, but there is a state contractors' board. And if you really believe that Dan is billing you unfairly, you have the right to register a complaint with the board. Just keep in mind, even if you win, it doesn't guarantee you much money. But, here's where the teeth are. If Dan can't prove that his fees are fair, there's a good chance he could lose his contractor's license."

"Really?"

"Yes, I hate to tell you this because I'd rather see you settle this with him out of court. It seems that no one really wins once you go to court. Of course, if you were willing, I could probably be a mediator between you two for some sort of dispute resolution."

"Oh, would you? Could you?"

"I can sure try."

"Thank you, Matthew. I really appreciate it."

"Sure, I'd be glad to help."

"Have you heard from Quin?" asked Holly.

Kestra shook her head and looked down. "I wouldn't be surprised if he didn't come back after all this craziness with Dan. He's probably concerned for his safety."

"That would be too bad. I really like that guy," said Matthew thoughtfully.

Kestra looked up. "Really? I mean, you hardly know him."

"Sometimes you can just tell what a guy is made of."

"I hope so. The truth is, I hardly know anything about him."

"Maybe. But I bet you know him better than you think."

32

Kestra pulled another narrow strip of old wallpaper from an upstairs bedroom. It was a slow and tedious process, but she was determined to finish before lunchtime. She had decided to invite Karen and Page to live with her. She would trade them room and board for work once the restaurant got started. That is, if she could even get it started. But she wouldn't think about that right now. She was determined to take life one day at a time, trusting God to take care of her. If he wanted her to have the Wise Man's House, he would have to work out the details.

She heard someone pull into the driveway and looked down to see Dan's pickup. What was he doing here? Hopefully he was not delivering a lien. She continued to peel off paper, hoping that if she ignored him, he might just go away. But the next thing she knew his voice was echoing through her house. Just who did he think he was, walking right in as if he owned the place?

She went to see what he wanted, praying to control her temper with each step.

"I didn't hear you knock," she began.

"Sorry about that."

"What do you want?"

He looked around. "Looks like you've had some work done?"

"Just some friends helping out."

He nodded. "Well, I was passing by and I wanted to check on you. I wanted to say again how sorry I am that things have gotten to this place."

"What place?"

"You know, all this trouble about money and everything. I just thought maybe you and I should sit down and talk it all over, see if we can come to some agreement."

She remembered Matthew's suggestion. "That sounds good, Dan. Maybe we could have a mediator. Matthew said—"

"Oh, I don't think we need a mediator, Kestra. Why don't we give it a try first? Just you and me. We've been friends for a long time. We ought to be able to work this out." He leaned over and patted Riley and smiled. "How you doing there, buddy?"

Kestra stared at him. Was this the same guy? What was he trying to pull here? "I don't know, Dan. This is a pretty serious situation. I don't think it can be solved so—"

"Come on, Kestra. I think we can work it out. Won't you give it a try? I really want to see you keep this house. I know how much it means to you. You've put so much into it."

She studied his face. He seemed sincere. "Okay, Dan, I guess it can't hurt to talk." She started to come down the stairs.

"I'd like to talk right now, Kestra, but I've got a job to bid in about twenty minutes. Can I come back over afterwards?"

"Sure. That would be fine, I guess."

He smiled up at her with that choirboy look.

"See ya later, then." He waved and left, and she wondered if she'd be sorry. Maybe she should call Matthew. But then maybe this was better, maybe she could make Dan understand.

She got the wallpaper stripped off the two rooms by five and Dan still hadn't returned. She did a quick clean up and went downstairs to fix a sandwich. What was taking him so long anyway? She wanted to hurry and get this done and over with. It would probably just be a waste of time anyway.

She checked her answering machine, praying to find a message from Quin. How she longed to hear his voice. But there were no calls. She'd been using it for a week now and couldn't remember it ever having a single call on it. Did the stupid thing even work? Just then she heard Riley barking and someone knocking at the door.

It was Dan. But it looked like he'd gone home and cleaned up. And he had roses; at least a dozen red roses, all neatly arranged in a beautiful crystal vase.

"These are for you."

"Why? What for?" she stammered, opening the door and leading him into the library.

"Well, for one thing, I owe you a vase." He looked down at his hands. "I really am sorry about that. I was so jealous, I just couldn't see straight."

"This vase is much nicer than the one you broke." She set the roses on the table and sat on the edge of a chair across from the sofa. She didn't want to be too close to him. Something didn't feel right about this visit.

"Kestra, I don't know how things have gotten so bad between us. I want to make them right." When he looked into her eyes, it almost seemed as if there were tears in his.

"So do I."

"I heard that Quin left."

"Yes, well, but not for good…"

His eyebrows lifted. "Oh, really, do you know that for sure?"

"No, not for sure."

He nodded. "Well, I didn't come to talk about him. I want to talk about us."

"Us?" Kestra took in a quick breath.

"Kestra, you know that I love you. I've always loved you. You've always been the only one for me."

"Even when you married Melinda?"

"I've already explained that. It was a big mistake that I have paid for again and again."

She shook her head slowly. It was like a strange dream. The conversation was all wrong. "Dan, please I've told you already, there is no 'us.' I thought we were going to talk about the house. The situation…"

"Right, Kestra. I understand, and I have come up with the perfect solution."

"Yes?" she answered eagerly.

"Marry me. And we will never have to worry about who owes what on the house. Please, Kestra, just marry me. I love you. I'm sorry for the fool that I've been. Marry me, Kestra, and we'll put all that nonsense behind us."

She was stunned. What made him think he could just come in here and propose—as though that would solve everything! She remembered her prayer not to lose her temper. She closed her eyes and prayed it again, silently, sincerely.

"Kestra," he spoke her name softly. She opened her eyes and he was actually kneeling right next to her chair, looking up with pleading eyes. He placed his hand on hers. "Kestra, did you hear me? What are you doing?"

She stared at him in total disbelief. "Praying," she said in barely a whisper. She pulled her hand away and tried not to show how horrified she felt.

He smiled. "Good. Now, I don't want you to answer right now. I know you must be pretty shocked. And I understand. But I want you to think about it. Think about how much I love you. For how long I've loved you. Remember how it used to be Kestra, back in high school when we were close. Think about how wonderful it would be for us to finish this house together. I could do everything you've always dreamed of. This house could be totally amazing. Just think about everything, and I'll call you in the morning." He stood and quickly left before she could even formulate the words.

She paced the room like a caged animal. Of course she would never marry him! Not under any conditions! There was nothing to think about. Nothing to consider. It was insane! Why hadn't she just yelled "NO!"? Why had she allowed him to leave without an answer?

Where was Quin? She had known this would happen—it was too good to last. Just when she was ready to completely put her trust in him—he had abandoned her. Just like her father had done. Just like Jack.

She sat down and stared at the roses. Red. For true love. She knew she didn't love Dan. She would never love him. Yet was it possible that something in her longed for such an escape? Was some pitiful part of her looking for the easy way out? The thought sickened her. Was she that weak?

"God, please help me!" she cried. "I am so confused. I thought you led me to this house. I believed you wanted me to have it. Now it looks like I'm losing it. Losing everything..." She leaned back and closed her eyes. She waited. She prayed...

After a while, she was filled with an unexplainable peace. She stood and picked up the crystal vase and roses. She carried them through the kitchen and out the back door. She took the lid off the trash can and dropped them in, vase and all.

"I would rather live in a shack with peace," she proclaimed as she fastened the lid closed. She looked up at the Wise Man's House illuminated by the last rose-colored sunrays. "Thank you, Lord. I know you'll take care of me."

～ 33 ～

She spent the next day hanging fresh wallpaper in one of the spare bedrooms. She tried not to replay the sound of Dan's angry voice last night when she had called him. She had calmly and politely told him that she could never marry him—would never marry him, no matter what. He had hung up. She felt a little bit sorry for him, but mostly relieved.

She smoothed out another strip of paper. She liked the cool feel of the slightly damp paper as it adhered to the wall. She used a wet sponge to work out another bubble and then stepped back to admire the pale blue and cream stripes. She hoped this room might be used by Page. She hadn't told Page and Karen of this plan yet. She wanted to get the rooms all done first.

Finally, just as the sun set, she hung the last strip. She dropped the sponge into the bucket and stood and stretched. She looked around the room. Not half bad. The stripes were fairly straight. At least as straight as the old walls would allow. It was a very pleasant room. She hoped Page would like it.

Poor Riley had been begging for a walk all evening, and now he was darting back and forth in the hallway, wagging his tail nervously.

"Okay, boy, I'm ready to go now." She followed him down-stairs, and as soon as she opened the door he burst out and began to bark wildly.

"What is it, Riley?" she asked, glancing around. "Do you hear something?" It was still light enough to see, and she saw nothing out of the ordinary. Except—was that a light coming from the cottage? Could it be that Quin had finally returned? She walked toward the cottage, cautiously looking around as she went. She was still a little worried about how Dan might react to her most recent rejection. When she got near enough, she peeked around the side to see the Land Rover parked neatly in its spot.

After a brief momentary sigh of relief, she was suddenly and unexpectedly filled with a raging anger. Why had he never called her, or even written a quick note? Here she had been going through all these horrible trials, and he didn't even have the decency to pick up the phone. She marched up his steps and pounded loudly on his door, ready to let him have it. He opened the door with a startled look, then broke into a warm smile.

"Where were you?" she demanded. "Where have you been? Why didn't you call?"

"What do you mean? Didn't you get my messages?"

"What messages?"

"I left several on that machine of yours."

She didn't know what to say. She hadn't gotten them, but then again she had never been very good with electronic devices. Come to think of it, maybe there wasn't even a tape in the machine. She'd have to check. "But you didn't even tell me you were going."

"I'm trying to tell you. I called. I left some messages. But let's skip that. First of all, I was in New York—"

"Why? What were you doing there?"

"Signing a book contract." He smiled. "Care to come in?

She walked in and continued the inquisition. "So you're a writer. Is that it? Why couldn't you just tell me that before?"

"You never asked."

"But you were so secretive."

"You're right, I was. At first. Then I practically begged you to ask me about myself."

She bit her lip. She knew it was true. "But by then it was too difficult. I didn't even know where to start. I guess I was afraid..."

"I know. I should have just come out and told you about myself."

"Yes, and why didn't you want me to know you were a writer? Do you write bad books or something?"

He laughed. "I sure hope not." He took her hands in his and looked into her face. "Kestra, I wanted you to love me for who I am, not for what I do."

"Why should it make any difference what you do?" She looked into his eyes and wondered why it made any difference now. He had mentioned the word *love!* Now all he had to do was kiss her and she would forget everything else.

"Come and sit down, let me explain."

They sat on the couch and he continued to hold her hands, looking deeply into her eyes as he told his story.

"You see, I was engaged to a woman, Helen. She told me that she loved me, and I thought I loved her. But when it was all said and done, it turned out she loved the image of me. She imagined that because I'm a writer, we would lead this amazing and exciting life. She was so captivated by how she thought we would live—constantly going places, meeting people and all— that she had no clue what my life was really like. When she discovered that I need solitude to work, and that I'm really quite hermit-like by nature, and that I'd rather not be the life of the party, well, you know…"

Kestra smiled. "I know."

"And when I first met you, I could tell that you were accustomed to something of a glamorous lifestyle. I was so certain that history was repeating itself that I started to pull completely out of the picture. But I couldn't get you out of my mind, so I decided to come back and to proceed with caution, to allow you to know me, warts and all."

"And those things, the things that you describe as 'warts'—those are things I already know about you. And I already—" She stopped herself.

"There's more." His face was wonderfully close to hers now. How she wished he would quit talking and just kiss her. "Remember Patrick O'Riley?"

"Of course," she murmured with a sigh.

"Remember that great-grandson of his?"

Suddenly she sat up straight and pulled her hands away. "No!" she said, stunned.

He nodded.

"No, you're kidding me! You're just teasing me, aren't you, because you know how much I love him?"

He stood and walked over to a stack of papers laid out on his old leather briefcase. He picked one up and pointed to the name on it.

She read it out loud. "James Q. O'Riley? What about Quin Larson? I thought your name was Quin Larson."

"James Quin Larson. But I use O'Riley as my pen name in honor of my great-grandfather."

She shook her head in disbelief. "That's why you had all his books."

"So, now you know the whole truth. Do you still love me?"

"Who said I love you?"

"You don't have to."

And finally, at long last, he pulled her into his arms and leaned down and kissed her! He kissed her with longing, with force mixed with tenderness. And with passion. She didn't even notice if his beard tickled or not because it felt like she was floating high over the earth. It felt like fireworks were exploding inside her, and she never wanted it to end.

When they finally pulled away, it was with difficulty. She knew she could be comfortable in his arms for the rest of her life.

She smiled up at him. "So, are there any other secrets I should be aware of."

The corners of his eyes crinkled ever so slightly. "Maybe…"

Her eyes widened. "Oh?"

"I guess I have one more very small confession to make. Do you remember when there was someone else trying to buy the Wise Man's House?"

She looked up in surprise. "I knew it! It was you after all!"

He grinned sheepishly, then gently pushed a tendril of hair away from her face. "When you told me about your childhood memories, and then about your dream to buy and restore this house, I knew I couldn't take that from you, and I backed out of my offer."

"So you really did want this house, almost as much as I did?"

He nodded.

"And you gave it up for me?"

He nodded again. "And now I'm hoping you'll let me share your dream with you…"

She threw her arms around him. "You're already a big part of it!"

"I love you, Kestra. I fell for you right from the start. Remember the day I almost scared you off the rock wall?" He pulled her toward him again.

"I love you, Quin. I love you with my whole heart, and I know I always will." They kissed again. But this time, they both heard an explosion.

They ran over to the window to see the sky light up with orange flames shooting out of the carriage house. They both burst out the door. The carriage house was already engulfed in explosive flames, and a strong wind had begun to send sparks directly toward the stables.

"The horses!" cried Kestra.

"I'll let them out, you go call for help!"

Kestra raced for the house and grabbed the phone. As she was yelling her address, she thought she saw someone streak by the back of the house. She hung up and dashed back to help Quin. By the time she reached the stable, it, too, was on fire. Quin led Annie out and safely away from the flame, then slapped her on the flank to set her running. Then he ran back for the others.

In the meantime, Kestra grabbed up the nearby hose and turned it on full blast. She doused the flames wherever she could reach and watched in fear as Quin pulled the horses out one by one. Finally, he went in for the last one; it was Othello. But the high-strung horse reared and flailed his hooves in fright.

"Be careful," she yelled as she saw a mighty hoof come down. But it was too late.

"Quin!" she screamed as he crumpled to the ground. The frightened horse ran off into the night and Kestra ran and kneeled by Quin's side.

"Quin, speak to me! Are you okay?" He did not answer, and the flames were growing hotter, more intense. "Help me, God," she prayed as she grabbed Quin by both arms and tried to pull him away from the flames. But he was a dead weight. "Take this house, God," she cried. "Take the horses, take everything, just please, God, don't take Quin!" The heat burned blistering hot on her back, it felt like her shirt was melting as she lay herself across his limp body.

Suddenly, strong arms lifted her and pulled her away from Quin. She turned to see Dan Hackett!

"No, Dan!" she screamed. "Leave me alone!" She would rather die with Quin than be saved by Dan. But Dan's strength was greater than hers.

"No, Dan, leave me alone!" she screamed as she beat against him with her fists.

"Kestra, I'm trying to help you!"

She continued to scream and fight as he dragged her away from the smoke and flames. "Leave me alone! I want to stay with Quin!"

"Kestra!" he yelled. "If you don't quit fighting, I won't be able to help Quin!"

She stopped flailing and looked into his face.

"Trust me," he said as he set her firmly on the ground a safe distance away from the fire. How could she trust him after all he had done? Perhaps, had even set the fire!

The stable was completely engulfed now and the heat was excruciating. Dan returned to Quin, bending down. She watched in horror. What would he do? To her amazement he picked up Quin and carried him over to her and lay him on the ground.

"Thank you, Dan. Thank you," she sobbed as she held Quin in her arms.

She leaned her face down to Quin's and saw that he was breathing evenly. But still he remained unconscious. She looked up to see Dan staring at her with a puzzled expression. Then he turned and walked away. Kestra's eyes followed him as he picked up the still running hose and began dousing the flames with it. What had Dan been doing here this time of night? And why had he helped them? Kestra heard sirens in the distance and soon fire trucks began to arrive and paramedics rushed over to tend to Quin and Kestra. Quin regained consciousness on the way to the hospital, and other than a lump on the head and some burns, he seemed to be fine. They were both treated for shock and burns and released early the next morning.

Holly and Matthew silently drove them back to the house. Kestra expected to find nothing more than smoldering ashes. But she didn't care. At least she still had Quin.

To her surprise, the Wise Man's House was still standing. Only the south wing appeared to have sustained damage. The carriage house and the stable were both gone.

"Hi, Kestra," called Page as the four got out of the car. She had black soot smeared across her cheek and looked tired. "I rounded up the horses. They're all okay. Othello had a minor burn, but I've put some antibiotic ointment on it. They're all in the pasture now. I'm sure sorry about your losses, Kestra. But I'm thankful you're okay."

"Thanks." Kestra gave her a hug. "Thanks for all your help."

"Morning, Ms. McKenzie," called out the fire chief as he walked up. "I've got a crew investigating. Any ideas about how it could have started?"

Kestra looked at Quin. She had already told him about the person she had seen run by the back of the house, and then about the strange occurrence when Dan rescued them.

"The lady has gone through quite a bit in the last twelve hours," said Quin. "Why don't you give her a chance to unwind, and if we think of anything, we'll be sure to let you know."

She looked up at Quin as the fire chief walked back to his crew. "Thanks, Quin. I appreciate it." It seemed unthinkable that it could be arson, and yet the circumstances were so strange, and Dan had been so angry about the rejection.

Quin seemed to read her thoughts and put a protective arm around her. "We don't need to figure this out right now. Let's go inside and make some coffee."

"I'm just going inside to start some," announced Holly as she and Matthew went on ahead.

Kestra lingered for a moment, looking at the black, smoldering piles of wood where buildings had once stood. It was sad, but it could have been so much worse. Kestra breathed a prayer of thanks and turned toward the house.

"We found the source," called one of the firemen. "Looks like some faulty wiring in the carriage house ignited the whole thing." He held up a glob of dark melted wires.

Kestra turned to Quin. "So Dan didn't—"

"No, I didn't."

Kestra spun around to see Dan walking up from behind. Quin turned and took a step toward Dan, his hand outstretched. Dan hesitated, but only for a moment, then he extended his hand.

"Thanks, Dan," said Quin with a serious smile. He patted Dan on the back. "You saved my life."

Dan nodded with a firm jaw. "I did it for Kestra." He looked at her with sad eyes and continued. "I don't really blame you for suspecting me, Kestra. I know I've been a real pain lately." He slowly shook his head, eyes downcast. "I don't know what to say, except that I'm real sorry about everything."

Kestra stepped up and placed her hand on Dan's arm. "It's okay, Dan. And just for the record, I really didn't think you could do something like this." She glanced over at the charred remains of the burned buildings.

"It's too bad," said Dan.

"But it could have been worse," said Kestra glancing up at Quin. "Much, much worse." Quin smiled and put an arm around her. Kestra turned back to Dan. "And I will always be grateful for what you did last night, Dan. Thank you for saving Quin."

Dan nodded grimly, then cleared his throat. "I've decided to get away for a while. I need some space to clear my head." He looked at Kestra, a sad trace of longing still in his eyes. "I've been trying way too hard to have things my way, without caring about who gets hurt. Matthew's been helping me to see things a little more clearly. And now I need to straighten some things out. It's about time I started taking God more seriously. Matthew says that God has a plan for my life." Dan sighed and shook his head. "Although it's pretty hard to believe that God could actually salvage anything out of my mess."

"You'd be surprised, Dan," said Kestra.

"Yes," agreed Quin. "I've seen God do some pretty amazing things."

"Well, I hope you're right." Dan looked right at Quin. "Take care of her," he said in a quiet but firm voice.

"I will," said Quin, his arm tightening protectively around Kestra's shoulders. Dan started to turn and walk away.

"Dan," called Kestra.

He turned and looked at her, it seemed there were tears in his eyes.

"I'll be praying for you—" she said, her voice breaking at the end. He nodded and walked away. Unexpected tears began to stream down her cheeks. She turned to Quin. "I thought I'd be so happy to see him leave, once and for all. But I feel so sorry for him. I hope he'll be okay."

"God is watching over him," said Quin.

"But I feel sort of guilty, maybe if I had just—"

Quin bent down and stopped her words with a kiss, and suddenly all the world's troubles faded. They slowly pulled away, and Quin took her by the hand, turning toward the house.

"Now, let's get down to business," said Quin as they walked. "No offense, Kestra, but it looks like you can't quite pull off this business venture. I think you need a partner to help you run the Wise Man's House." He stopped and pulled her close again.

"Well, just for your information, I happen to have very good fire insurance!"

"I always knew you were one smart businesswoman, Kestra McKenzie."

"Thank you." She smiled.

"How about it though? Are you willing to let me help you? Can we rebuild this house together? Will you marry me, Kestra?"

She threw her arms around him. "I thought you would never ask!"

Quin smiled down at her and chuckled. "Well, if I want to live in the Wise Man's House, maybe it's about time I started to act accordingly."

"Quin, I've always thought of you as one of the wisest people I have ever known," she said softly.

The corners of his eyes crinkled and he pulled her close. "Spending the rest of my life with you is the wisest thing I could ever do!"

As Quin kissed her and held her close, she thanked God for bringing them together. To think the great God of the universe would take time to answer her prayers and fulfill her childhood dreams went far and beyond her wildest imaginings. Forever more her life, like the Wise Man's House, would be built upon him!

Dear Reader,

Most of my favorite childhood memories can be found along various parts of the beautiful Oregon coast. And consequently it has become a familiar setting for many of my books.

Long ago, even before Palisades was a series, I began writing *Wise Man's House*. At that time, my family and I were fully immersed in a house building project ourselves, and it was easy to understand Kestra's passion and frustration when all did not go smoothly.

Since that time, I've become a full-time editor at Questar Publishers. And not surprisingly, as I finished this book I found my family once again immersed in a building project. This time it's a major renovation.

In other words, I tend to write from my life.

You may wonder—how can romance and renovation live under the same roof? It's not easy! Love takes careful tending, good communication, and lots of forgiveness. Any serious building or remodeling project can put even the best relationship to the test.

But life is like that for "romantics." It seems we constantly need to balance our desire for beauty and perfection against the reality of keeping people first and loving each other unselfishly. And although it's not easy, the challenge can be very rewarding and fulfilling.

My hope is that you'll enjoy this book and remember that "Unless the Lord builds the house, its builders labor in vain" (Psalm 127:1).

Blessings!

Melody A. Carlson

PALISADES...PURE ROMANCE